CALLED BY NAME

Called by Name

THE INSPIRING STORIES OF 12 MEN WHO BECAME CATHOLIC PRIESTS

EDITED BY

Christine Anne Mugridge and Jerry Usher

FOREWORD BY

Most Reverend Donald Wuerl, D.D., S.T.D.,
Archbishop of Washington

ASCENSION PRESS

West Chester, Pennsylvania

Ascension Press
Post Office Box 1990
West Chester, PA 19380
Orders: 1-800-376-0520
www.AscensionPress.com

Cover design: Kinsey Caruth

Printed in the United States of America
07 08 09 10 11 12 8 7 6 5 4 3 2 1

ISBN 978-1-934217-36-8

*This book is dedicated to all those men
whom God is calling to be His priests.*

*May "He who began the good work in you ...
bring it to completion at the day
of Jesus Christ" (Philippians 1:6).*

Contents

FOREWORD

Often at the conclusion of Mass in one of our parishes, I will remind the faithful of our need to encourage vocations. I point out that in their parish there have to be young people whom God is calling to religious life and, specifically, to the priesthood. Since the voice of God quietly touches the heart, we can assume that the one hearing this call will want to talk to someone about it and the prospects of serving Christ. I ask our faithful to encourage young people to consider the possibility of becoming a religious or a priest. At the same time, I challenge parishioners to identify young people in the parish who show some signs of a possible vocation and ask them to think about helping to do the work of Jesus in his Church. I try to conclude with the reminder that the one thing we can all do is pray that God will touch the hearts of our young people to be open to his call.

At a recent gathering sponsored by our local Serra Club honoring our newly ordained, I listened to testimony after testimony that highlighted how important it is that we encourage young people to think about the possibility of a call from God in their lives. All of the newly ordained who spoke could clearly recall the impact that a challenging question, pointing out the possibility of their vocation, had for them.

God calls each of us. In one way or another the call comes. It is God who invites us to respond generously and so to find true joy in opening our hearts to God's grace. "My grace is sufficient for you, for my power is made perfect in weakness" (2 Corinthians 12:9). In the marvel of God's plan each of us is called to walk with Jesus on the journey that will bring us to the knowledge of God in this life and to eternal joy with God in the life to come.

The real challenge begins when we hear the quiet voice of the Lord calling to us: "Friend, come closer" (Luke 14:10). Some are called to serve Christ as his priest. The call from God can come to us in prayer, through the words of Sacred Scripture. It can reach us in all manners of ways—through literature, through human love, through happiness or suffering or both, through the unconscious witness of some holy friend, through a sudden outpouring of compassion for another.

Called by Name is a collection of vocational stories. It speaks of the lives, call, and response of a number of bishops and priests who heard the call, were encouraged to pursue it, and were fortified during the entire discernment and vocation process by the support and prayers of so many others. *Called by Name* is a welcome reminder that it is God who calls us. "It was not you who chose me, but I who chose you" (John 15:16). This book recalls how wonderfully blessed are those who respond to the call, embrace it, and live it. This highly readable book is a credible invitation rooted in the lived experience of happy priests to open one's heart to the joy and wonder of God's call.

My hope is that this book will be an inspiration to young people searching their own hearts to determine what God asks of them. May it also be a reminder that each of us has to do our part in identifying people whom God might be calling so that we can offer them our encouragement and our prayers. Ultimately, since God's call is a work of the Holy Spirit, our part in encouraging vocations will always include prayer. Perhaps as we go through these stories that speak of the fruit of the response to God's call, we will all be reminded to pray all the more fervently that the next generation of spiritual leadership in the Church will hear and respond generously to this call.

—Most Reverend Donald W. Wuerl, D.D., S.T.D.,
Archbishop of Washington

INTRODUCTION

In his final annual letter to his brother priests written from Gemelli Hospital in Rome, March 13, 2005, John Paul II writes in part of Christ's self-giving and of the corresponding thanksgiving which characterize the Eucharistic Celebration and the life of the priest:

> Christ's self-giving, which has its origin in the Trinitarian life of the God who is Love, reaches its culmination in the sacrifice of the Cross, sacramentally anticipated in the Last Supper. It is impossible to repeat the words of consecration without feeling caught up in this spiritual movement. In a certain sense, when he says the words: "take and eat," the priest must learn to apply them also to himself, and to speak them with truth and generosity. If he is able to offer himself as a gift, placing himself at the disposal of the community and at the service of anyone in need, his life takes on its true meaning. This is exactly what Jesus expected of his apostles... It is also what the People of God expect of a priest.[1]

What do we think of when we hear the word, "priest"? What are our expectations; our thoughts on the true meaning of such a life? Scandals notwithstanding, the Lord continues to call and anoint men to this formidable vocation. For the People of God, this life of self-giving is a manifestation of God's mercy on earth. The bottom line seems to be that each priest, with all his human strengths and weaknesses, is called to commit to living

---

[1] John Paul II, *Letter of the Holy Father John Paul II to Priests for Holy Thursday 2005* (Vatican City: Libreria Editrice Vaticana, 2005), no.3.

in the image of Christ—that is, *in persona Christi*—so that all
of humanity may be caught up in the great salvific love of the
Triune God who manifests His grace on earth in a manner most
excellent in the Real Presence. John Paul writes that deepening
faith and joy spring from our participation in this heavenly
Communion:

> Gratitude is the disposition which lies at the root of the
> very word "Eucharist." This expression of thanksgiving
> contains the whole Biblical spirituality of praise for
> the *mirabilia Dei*. God loves us, he goes before us in his
> Providence, and he accompanies us with his continuous
> saving acts. In the Eucharist Jesus thanks the Father with
> us and for us. How could this thanksgiving of Jesus fail to
> shape the life of a priest?" He knows that he must cultivate
> *a constant sense of gratitude* for ... the gift of faith, which it
> is his task to proclaim, and for the gift of the priesthood,
> which consecrates him totally to the service of the Kingdom
> of God. We have our crosses to bear—and we are certainly
> not the only ones!—but the gifts we have received are so
> great that we cannot fail to sing from the depths of our
> hearts our own *Magnificat*.[2]

God loves us, goes before us and continues to accompany
us. Certainly His greatest gift of love is that of Himself, truly
present in the most Holy Eucharist. With this knowledge, each
person who shares in this great Sacrament is called to live with
a constant sense of gratitude for such a gift. This gift is made
manifest through the hands of the priest. The praise and glory
belong to the Lord, yes. But it is only right and just to pause and
give a special note of gratitude not only for each of the priests
whose stories are told in this book but for every priest. We
acknowledge and give thanks for this mysterious and merciful
gift of God to the Church.

---

[2] John Paul II, *Letter of the Holy Father John Paul II to Priests for Holy Thursday
2005* (Vatican City: Libreria Editrice Vaticana, 2005), no. 2.

Each of us may recall a special priest in our lives who has been both *celebrant* and *guardian* of the faith: the one whose consoling words at a particularly difficult confession brought us true emotional freedom; the pastor who simply "was there" with a smile and heartening word during the ups and downs of family life; or the priest assigned to serve the young adult group, touching the hearts and minds of young men and women in a manner that kept them on the right track. Some of us are familiar with the extraordinary phrase of St. Pio of Pietrelcina (Padre Pio) in which he notes, "It would be easier for the world to exist without the sun than without the Holy Sacrifice of the Mass." Are we not amazed and most grateful as we think of the millions of souls throughout the centuries who have received the Lord's saving grace (and mercies untold) through participation in the Holy Mass? How else are we to respond but with an overwhelming sense of awe and gratitude for such a marvelous gift? The knowledge that our Lord Jesus Christ entrusts Himself to us with great humility in the Blessed Sacrament through the hands of the priest at each Mass should likewise inspire a respect and joy for these brave apostles today.

This project was originally inspired by the life-witness and teaching of John Paul II, who himself recalled the gift of the laity and their contribution to the growth of his priesthood. As laity, we are inspired by what John Paul referred to as the "the urgent need for the apostolate of the laity in the Church" spoken of by the Second Vatican Council in terms of *vocation and mission*.[3] The effort to begin collaboration on this project was motivated by a conversation that took place nearly ten years ago about the great gift and mystery of the priesthood. We felt a strong desire to refresh the love within the People of God for their priests and to assist in awakening a new generation of men to the call of the Lord.

---

[3] John Paul II, *Gift and Mystery* (Boston: Daughters of St. Paul, 1996), p. 84.

Once the overall concept for the book took shape, the question naturally arose, "How to choose those priests who would share their testimony?" St. Paul indicates in his letter to the Corinthians that a priest is a servant of Christ, a steward of the mysteries of God and must be found trustworthy (1 Cor 4:1-2). We sought the participation of men who were fully aware of their priest-servant identity, zealous in living out their priesthood as custodians of the treasures of our faith, conscious of this great responsibility and open to sharing their lives' stories for the purpose of encouraging others to the vocation. During the process of interviewing the priests and editing their stories, we found that God's call is indeed divinely mysterious, manifesting itself in a multiplicity of ways in the life of each individual. As you will read, each man's call was quite personal from the Lord, echoing in the depths of his heart with a sense of fear, joy and deep knowing.

St. Thérèse of Lisieux once said, "God does not call those who are worthy, but those whom it pleases Him to call." We were blessed by the attitude of humility from each of the priests who agreed to share their stories. In fact, being put up on a pedestal was the last thing they wanted! Our awareness of the precious gift of the priesthood and amazement at the courage of each man's "yes" to the call of Christ grew as we realized how vulnerable a man is during this walk of faith in his vocation— and in sharing this faith walk with others. Finally, as talented and admirable as each of these priests is, we were reminded of the uniquely beautiful truth that there is only one priesthood, only one Priest, Jesus Christ. It is in and through the priesthood of Jesus Christ that His priests are called to live.

This final collected work is presented to the reader with the hope that it will encourage a sense of gratitude and thanksgiving, not only for the men who have shared their stories here but for the gift of the priesthood throughout the world. How many thousands of wonderful priests are living in places unknown whose stories are unheard? We dedicate this book to these priests, without whom the world would be lost. We may ask, "How many of these priests need our support and solidarity as members of the Body of Christ? Further still, how many men who are being called to the priesthood today need the prayerful encouragement of us all? We hope that those men who are inspired by the Lord to the vocation of the priesthood, will be encouraged to give of themselves without reservation. Likewise, let us join together in prayer for these and all those whom Christ is calling to the priesthood; a call like no other.

—Christine Mugridge and Jerry Usher
December 8, 2007
Solemnity of the Immaculate Conception

Written in entrustment to the Blessed Virgin Mary on the solemnity of her Immaculate Conception.

1

FROM LENIN TO OUR LADY

FR. MAXIM POPOV, CMF

"Papa, could God exist?" At only eight years old, it took all the nerve I could muster to ask that question. I was fearful of my father, especially to his reaction to my inquisitions about God.

An officer in the Soviet Army, Papa was also a descendent of a family of fervent believers of the ideals of communism and socialism. My mama was a theater director and cultural organizer. I had one sister, Julia, who was four years younger than me. We lived in the western Siberian city of Tomsk before moving to East Germany. Given the Soviet milieu, ours was a normal family.

I was a quiet but inquisitive child. I remember speaking with a soldier one day when I was very young. He explained that the sun would burn out within several million years. The thought of such a calamity distressed me greatly for I wondered what would become of the earth. I grieved for people and all living things that would inevitably perish. Then, I told myself, "This is the way it has to be in life. Everything has to end sometime." Yet I still felt helpless in the face of this mystery of complete annihilation and death.

My father taught me to read before I entered the first grade, so I read a lot about the hero I admired most, Vladimir Lenin. Once in school, I was thrilled to find an enormous portrait of Lenin hanging on the wall of my first grade classroom. Beneath it was the phrase, *Lenin lived. Lenin lives. Lenin will live.* I was able to read it but unable to comprehend its meaning. How could a person live simultaneously in the past, present, and future? In my final analysis, I settled for the simple answer, "That's Lenin."

I will never forget the day in first grade when I became an Oktyabrist, the first stage of initiation into the socialist structure.[1] I sprinted home from school proudly sporting a small red star with a portrait of Lenin on the lapel of my school uniform jacket. At just seven years old, I had received the coveted symbol that marked my family's core identity. Mama turned away from her cleaning when she saw me come near. Her prideful expression embraced me and she wrapped her arms around me affectionately.

We moved to East Germany in 1979 after my father was given a new assignment with the Soviet Army. It was around this time that I had begun sensing an incomprehensible "presence" during moments of silence and solitude. It first became apparent one afternoon when I stopped in front of the fence that surrounded a Catholic church while walking home from school. A warm peaceful aura emanated from the depths of my heart and engulfed my entire being. I felt loved, but for the life of me I could not figure out who or what this presence was. I only knew that I wanted to remain in that blessed state as long as possible. I cannot recall how long I stayed there leaning on the fence with my palms joined together before I was rudely awakened by the voice of a lady who knew my family. "You, the son of Popov, praying?" she said. "I'm going to tell your father!"

Praying? Aside from being told that He did not exist, I knew nothing about God. However, the thought of my father finding out that I had been lingering outside a church sprang forth my first consciously articulated prayer. *Lord, if you exist, don't let that lady say anything to papa!* When I returned home there was no incident, no scandal; therefore, I felt that I could speak with "the presence." Thus began a series of many conversations with

---

[1] The name comes from the Communist Revolution, which took place in
     October 1917

God about everything, and with no distinction between *sacrum et profanum*. It appeared that God answered my petitions, too. This was my most intimate secret. I loved to be in the company of the Presence at both difficult and joyous times.

Unlike most Russian military families, we lived among the Germans in a civilian neighborhood. I studied at a Russian school, but I played with German children so I was able to pick up the language rather quickly. I was also free to roam about town. Often, I would go to the center of East Berlin to sit in the Cathedral of St. Hedwig. I so loved to listen to the organ music and observe the priests. Even though I did not understand the sacredness of their actions, I felt at home.

I brought my mother to the church one day, hoping that she would share my admiration. Sadly, this did not happen. We conducted ourselves inappropriately during the Mass, laughing audibly at the priests, disrupting the service, and drawing attention to ourselves. Afterward, I felt very bad about it but I could not give my mother any indication that the beginnings of faith had appeared in me.

Another time, when my father and I were out walking alone, I posed the question about God to him. I was desperate for some sort of affirmation from my family. Instead, I faced further torment. "What do you mean, Maxim?" He responded indignantly. "That's all concocted by ignorant and dim-witted people." So my secret longing for God remained enclosed in my heart.

LEARNING TO PRAY

Knowing the presence I felt was God, I began to develop a deep desire to learn how to pray. It seemed to me that in addition to conversation with God, I should perform some sort of gesture or action. Gradually, I worked out a method of praying by trial and error. One day we had a math test that necessitated a powerful prayer. I recalled how believers traced with their hands some sort of sign on their bodies. So when the Hymn of the Soviet Union blared over the radio, I stood up and, using the tips of my right thumb and fingers, proceeded to trace a star on my forehead, stomach, and shoulders. With that, I set off confidently for school.

That day, I flunked my math test, fought with my buddies, and got it good from my mom. This taught me that this kind of prayer did not pay. Despite several such unsuccessful attempts, the desire to pray did not leave me. It grew deeper.

Once my family left East Germany and returned home to the Soviet Union, visiting churches was completely off limits. During this time I had become a Pioneer activist, which was a communist youth organization for children between the ages of eleven and sixteen. As such, I once told my teacher that a classmate attended church and wore a cross. For this he was probably punished. Meanwhile, I frequented the library to read all the books I could find on atheism since religious literature was nowhere to be found. My method of learning about the Catholic Faith was to read about priests who had *left* Holy Orders. That is how eager I was to learn how to pray. Eventually I came to understand the nature of my shortcomings—Catholics prayed in Latin but I had been praying in Russian.

One of my schoolbooks, *Ogon (The Gadfly)*, was about a cardinal who had an illegitimate son who became a priest. Upon learning that his father was actually a cardinal, the priest abandoned the Faith and became a revolutionary. This book was precious to me because it contained a prayer in Latin—a Catholic prayer that began, *Dies irae, dies illa*. I copied down the Latin prayer and carried it with me everywhere. It helped me tremendously, despite being, as I found out later, the opening canticle of the Mass for the Dead. I was just happy to be praying like the Catholics prayed.

My parents divorced when I was fourteen, which only intensified the deep need for "home" that had been developing in me. I longed for the sense of peace and serenity that I had experienced in the church in East Germany. Following the revolution and subsequent prohibition on religion, a beautiful Catholic church that had been built with the donations of Polish exiles in my hometown of Tomsk was being used for various functions: a horse stable, an aviation club, and, finally, a planetarium. Hoping for some kind of encounter, I frequented the building but it was barren—no organ music, no Presence.

One frozen Siberian night in the exceedingly fresh, almost sweet air, I stood before the closed doors of the church. I had gone on foot dreaming that I would meet the Presence but the doors were locked. *There is no God,* I concluded. *After all, if you existed, would you allow me to search for you so long? Would you permit someone to suffer without any kind of reply? All I wanted was to pray, to be with you. Therefore, it must be true that you are a myth, a fiction, an illusion, the means to control ignorant and dull-witted people, as we were told.* Having come to this realization, something within me died. I lacked the strength and desire to weep and I considered myself the victim of monstrous self-deception. Slowly, I descended the hill on which the church was built, believing I was doing so once and for all. Little did I know that this physical descent would be symbolic of my falling into a spiritual abyss.

MEDICINE, *PERESTROIKA*, AND THE BAPTISTS

I began to live like the majority of my contemporaries, trying anything and everything in order to find love, understanding, and intimacy. Over time I noticed that the sinful life did not satisfy me. Experiencing a deep need for something spiritual, I engaged in a variety of popular practices like theosophy, various Eastern religions, and even bioenergy therapy. In doing so, I unearthed a demonic force from within that unwittingly led to self-serving actions and lustful desires. The experience contradicted the peace and serenity that I had known with the Presence. I was unable to recognize the right path but coherent enough to know that I was not on it. I desperately needed spiritual realities.

At that time I had already finished Eight Year School[2] and had been the first of my classmates to join the Komsomols, a communist organization for young adults. I became a Komsomol group leader while studying at a three-year medical school. Having enjoyed medicine immensely, I spent considerable time in hospitals. I worked on a medical squad for a year, and in a maternity ward for the better part of another year. Medicine captivated me, and I thought that I had finally found myself. I wanted to become a doctor.

Around this time, the late 1980s, *perestroika*[3] had already begun spreading across the Soviet Union. Under the aegis of Mikhail Gorbachev, local authorities slowly began to permit religious practices again. Walking about the city one night, I came upon an evangelical Baptist church. I stopped in during a service but experienced no sense of "home." For about six months, however, I attended their prayer meetings, listened to religious radio programs, and carried a Bible around with me, although I did not read it much. At the suggestion of the church leader, I publicly repented of my sinful life. My way of life had not changed much, but I gained some knowledge of sin and an understanding of Christian morality.

However, after demonstrating a few of my non-Christian spiritual practices for a fellow church member, I was asked by the pastor to leave the congregation. He had concluded that I was from Satan. So I transferred to another Baptist society in Tomsk where I was encouraged to join the choir and receive baptism. While there, I discovered that the Catholic Church had

---

[2]   Under the Soviet educational system, for children ages 7–14; followed by Middle School (ages 15–17).

[3]   Literally, "restructuring"; a time of loosening economic and political controls in the USSR.

been returned to the believers in the Soviet Union, and I was sufficiently intrigued enough to check this out.

ENCOUNTER WITH OUR LADY

Curious and confident, I entered a Catholic church. I was immediately attracted to a discussion group gathered on one side of the church. I approached their circle without the least bit of hesitation and informed them that the Baptist faith was all anyone ever needed. They politely told me to sit nearby and that they would speak with me later. I went where they had indicated and, when I lifted my head, my eyes fell upon an old picture of the Blessed Virgin Mary. For the first time in years, that old familiar sense of peace, clarity, and warmth swathed me. At that very moment I was certain *this is my place. This is my home!* More than an emotion, it was a profound belief.

The church, Our Lady Queen of the Most Holy Rosary, had just been returned to the Church a half year earlier and it did not have a permanent priest or celebrant. Two gentlemen, Marek Machuga of Poland and Vladimir Senchuk of Tomsk, who later became my mentors, led the prayer meeting that night. Marek was an extraordinary minister of the Eucharist and he invited me to participate in the Liturgy of the Word the following morning. I did not sleep a wink that night, for this would be my first liturgy as a believer.

When I arrived at the church, only four *babushkas*[4] and Marek were in attendance. Since I spoke Russian, he asked me to read a selection from Sacred Scripture, and he cloaked me in a white robe. Singing a song from Taize, in Latin, we proceeded to serve. Prior to stepping up to the lectern, another conviction came upon me, a strong feeling that *my place is in the church at the pulpit.* I did not understand this at all but resolved to contemplate

---

[4]   Russian grandmothers or elderly women.

it later. I was just so happy that the long-awaited peace had returned and that, at last, I was home.

My catechumenate lasted about six months. I received the sacrament of baptism with about twelve others on Christmas Eve 1991. The ceremony was serene and joyful. After the service, all of the newly baptized spent the entire night at the church since none of us had a Catholic family with which to celebrate Christmas. We gathered on the second floor above the sacristy, drank tea, and ate candy that Marek had brought from Poland. Each of us was disappointed that no relatives had come to our sacred baptism, yet with hearts full of peace, each took comfort in the midst of our newfound family of believers.

INTO THE FRAY!

An acolyte from the moment I came into the Church, the conviction that I should become a priest did not leave me. Simultaneously, however, I cherished my own plans to work in medicine and help others. Fr. Anton Gsell, who instructed me in the faith, was an ordinary but deeply spiritual man, someone to emulate. I knew that if I were to become a priest, I wanted to be like Fr. Anton. He was of German descent but Russian born and raised, and therefore, *svoi*—one of us. Fr. Anton exemplified the essence of being Catholic in Russia, compassionately bringing to the parish the full richness of the traditions of the Universal Church.

The idea of becoming a priest would not leave me, and even though I prayed, "No, no. Not now. It's too soon," I began to inquire about the path to priesthood. There wasn't a single seminary where the instruction took place in Russian, and the seminary in Riga[5] was no longer accepting Russian-speaking candidates. I was informed that in the early days of my parish's rebirth a young priest from the Congregation of

---

[5]   The capital of Latvia and the largest city in the Baltic states.

Claretian Missionaries had visited. Fr. Antonii Badura, CMF was responsible for the formation of young religious. I wrote to him and he responded quickly with an invitation to visit his monastery in Poland. I placed the invitation on a shelf. "Let it wait," I told myself. "Not now. Medicine first."

The center of the Catholic Church in Siberia was located in Novosibirsk and we had no bishop at the time. Fr. Anton sent me and another youth representative from the parish to a meeting with Francesco Cardinal Colasuonno, the papal nuncio, who had arrived in Novosibirsk. After the meeting, a group of us went to the Akademgorodok District, some eighteen miles from the city. I sat apart from the other men so I could spend time with the Lord. In my silence came a great peace and a strong assurance, *I need to go to that monastery.*

Returning to the group, I said, "Guys, I'm leaving!"

"Where to?"

"The monastery."

"The monastery *where?*"

"In Poland."

"You! We knew you were something else, but this is really . . . "

"Yeah. We'll see. By the end of February I'll already be in the monastery." I told them calmly.

With no money and no international passport, which was difficult to obtain at the time, I had no idea how I was going to make this happen but my decision was resolute. Like a true Russian, I plunged into the fray.

I called my mother, who was in Leningrad[6] pursuing her second advanced degree. Although she was aware that I had entered the Catholic Faith, she had not known the extent of my conviction. She may have been a bit shocked by the news, but like most mothers, she was more concerned with how I was doing rather than what I was doing.

"Mom, I'm leaving!"

---

[6] The city's name has since been restored to St. Petersburg.

"Where to?"

"To the monastery. In Poland."

"What?! Do you have any money?"

"No."

"Wait. I'll send you some."

Within two days I received the exact amount of money needed to pay for a one-way ticket. Later, mama expressed regret at having sent the money, but it was too late. I had already bought my ticket. Miraculously, I managed to get my passport within one week. Wearing my rabbit's fur cap and my father's army jacket, I set out for the far-off and unknown on February 23, 1992.

It was somewhat ironic that I left for Poland on the Day of the Soviet Army and Navy or "Red Army Day," because a Polish bishop had once described the Claretian missionaries as "Christ's Commandos." I said good-bye to my neighbors, who were busy celebrating, as all Russian men do, the "Defenders of the Fatherland." When I said I was going to the seminary, one of the men pulled me aside and privately recounted his life's story. After hearing his difficult and complicated tale, I felt as though I had heard a general confession. As a token of his gratitude, he and his wife accompanied me to the train station and bought me a bottle of vodka, which was a substantial gift during such difficult times.

En route to Moscow, where I was to catch a connecting train to Poland, I prayed a lot. The crime rate was high in the capital and I feared something bad would happen to me there. I also worried that I might not be able to negotiate the big station. Though I had traveled through Moscow with my parents almost every year for five years, when I got off the train and looked around, I did not know what to do next. A young man dressed in a light-blue uniform approached me and asked if he could help. He must have seen by the look on my face that I was lost. Without thinking, I told him where I was traveling. He took my suitcase and led me to the place where I was to board the train to

Poland. Oddly, I was not uncomfortable with this stranger, but I did wonder what he might want from me. He pointed out some empty seats in the station and sat with me until my train arrived. He did not speak much and when I spoke about the Lord God, he only smiled. When my train arrived, he saw me off to the car and quietly took his leave. I wondered about the man in the light-blue suit. Was he a guardian angel sent directly from above—an answer to my prayers?

During the twenty-six hour train ride from Moscow to Wroclaw, Poland, a man and his wife offered to share their food with me, but I turned it down saying that I was fasting. In reality, my pride kept me from accepting their generosity. I arrived in Wroclaw without incident, but regretted that I had not accepted the couple's food offering. Perhaps I had turned away help from another God-sent angel.

TIME TO ADJUST

The residents of Kryudlina Mala Monastery will long remember my early morning arrival on February 28, 1992. Without warning, a large dog that seemed to pop out of nowhere lunged at me with a voracious bark. Somehow I managed to avoid the creature and rang the monastery doorbell. After identifying myself, I was sent to Fr. Antonii.

Fr. Antonii Badura, CMF, had been portrayed to me as a great missionary and a man of tremendous spiritual strength. He was, after all, one of the first to brave Siberia and evangelize in our parish. So I expected to meet a tall man with a deep voice. Instead, I met a soft-spoken man who only stood about five-feet-eight. Entering the room where I had been waiting, Fr. Antonii said, "Isn't this a nice present? Today just happens to be my birthday." He thanked me for coming and inquired about my trip. I never would have guessed that our first meeting would be so cordial. I was raised differently and accustomed to curt and detailed questions, not comments like, "Make yourself at home."

"We're glad you are here." My first instruction was to go rest on the bed that had been designated for me.

As I ascended the stairs to my room, I heard a Marian hymn, *Jasna Gora Apel*, and I knew instantly that I was home. Tearfully, I came to see that I had received far more than I had given up. The unmerited gift I received was a heavy burden for a recalcitrant man. Accepting this undeserved and unconditional love helped me to live in the community of young brothers. Throughout my three-and-a-half-year residency at the novitiate house, many men, morally and spiritually superior to me, had passed through its doors. Father Antonii, however, saw something in me that I had not noticed in myself. Above all, he believed in me.

Some lessons I needed to learn were harder than others. One morning after breakfast I was sent to potato peeling detail in the cellar. Stubbornly, I refused and went to my room. After all, I was the son of intelligentsia, of good breeding. I was not about to partake in any such duty. That evening when I turned down my bed, I found potatoes everywhere. The next morning I quietly picked up my potato peeler and joined the others in the cellar.

THE BLESSED MOTHER REVISITED

Clearly, the Blessed Virgin was with me from the beginning of my spiritual journey, but my brief Protestant background had left me a bit reserved toward her. I had nothing against Mary; my heart simply was hesitant towards her.

I had been shown the Rosary following one of my early catechism lessons. An instructor superficially explained its prayers but I never felt the need to pray it until years later when I was in the monastery. An overwhelming desire to pray the Rosary awakened me at three in the morning. I did not have one with me so I improvised. Transferring 150 vitamin C pills from one small tray to another, I prayed the entire Rosary. Through these prayers, I discovered Mary, the "Mother of Simple Love." I realized that she would never hurt nor demand the impossible and that she is the antidote to pride—

and humility is a disposition needed if one is to put God first. She is the sign and example that, with God, anything is possible. I knew that through the love of her Immaculate Heart anyone could become a true child of God, and I accepted her as my spiritual mother.

Perhaps some of the difficulty I previously had had accepting Mary as my mother stemmed from my rigid, adult-like childhood. At a very young age, I was given numerous responsibilities and was treated like an adult by the adults in my life. As a child, I was accustomed to being a victim, passively accepting injury, pain and suffering. I now believe it to be the root cause of the many days my life seemed dark and bleak to me. Ordinarily, I direct my focus on Christ and I invoke the Holy Spirit in prayer, but during the most difficult times of my life, I run to Mother Mary.

GRACES AND HEARTACHES

The first year in the novitiate house was dedicated to human development and language study. During this time, I prayed for the conversion of my family. After four months, Fr. Antonii took me with him to Siberia. We traveled to Novosibirsk and then on to Krasnoyars, where the Catholic community of twenty people gathered in an apartment in the city's Solnichni Region. In need of priests and a permanent place to gather and pray, they were glad to see us.

I tried to help Fr Antonii in every way, including serving as an interpreter when he met with people. It never occurred to me that one day I would serve in this very place as a priest. But God gives vocations to the priesthood and religious life in response to the deep desires of peoples' hearts. When I saw how sincerely these people wanted to encounter God in the Church, I wanted more than ever to become a priest.[7]

---

[7] A church is being built near the very apartment where the original Krasnoyarsk Catholic community used to meet.

For two days Fr. Antonii and I visited Tomsk, where I saw my family. I was alienated and misunderstood by both my mother and my beloved sister, Julia, who both said that there was no God. They said that I was wasting my time. Try as I might, I could not defend nor vindicate God. I left my home heavy-hearted. An insurmountable wall had sprung up between my loved ones and me.

Returning to Poland, I began to pray again for my family's conversion, believing that all would work out according to God's will. I longed to communicate the life I had received as an unmerited gift. As I prayed for my family, I also interceded for my friends and acquaintances, asking that they might receive the gift of faith. As time went on, nothing changed. My mother could not accept the existence of a benevolent God. Julia loved me but always sided with our mother. Thus began a vicious cycle of prayer, hope, and disappointment upon returning home. The situation seemed futile, but I never gave up hope. I even asked others to pray.

We visited Tomsk and Krasnoyarsk again in the summer of 1992. This time, Fr. Piotr Liszka accompanied us and we met with Bishop Josef Werth, who had recently been appointed apostolic administrator of Siberia. "You know," Bishop Werth said, "If it were someone else, I would not have let him enter religious life. But in your case, I'll give you my blessing." *Why?* I wondered. *What did the bishop see in me?*

Fr. Piotr quickly prepared me for confirmation. I was among the first in our parish to receive the sacrament. At the time, I had met a group of evangelists from the Catholic charismatic renewal. Impressed by their joy, courage, and prayerfulness, I asked them to pray over me. After doing so, I felt an unusual lightness and received the charismatic gift of praying in tongues. This has helped me tremendously, especially during moments of spiritual aridity.

A GREAT SORROW AND GREAT JOYS

In addition to her physical beauty, my sister Julia was also highly intelligent. She completed two years of middle school (high school in Western culture) in just one year and had begun studying at the Faculty of Foreign Languages at the Pedagogical Institute when she was diagnosed with cancer. Her illness forced her to discontinue her studies midway through her first year. Again, I spoke to her about the love of God that I had discovered, and this time the seed took root. Following an operation, she requested baptism in the Catholic Church.

I spent as much time as I could praying with her in the hospital. I prayed for the gift of healing, and we memorized passages from sacred Scripture together. Our communal prayer took many interesting forms, from the Rosary and Bible reading to spontaneous charismatic prayers. A priest came to the hospital to hear her confession and celebrate Mass, and all who visited marveled at her great strength and courage in the face of suffering. When Julia was discharged from the hospital, I returned to Poland and officially began my novitiate. I felt the strength of my sister's prayers at that time.

One day, while praying in the chapel with my eyes closed, I had a vision of my family's apartment in Tomsk. It was filled with a golden light. From my heart came the startling words, *If Julia dies that would be good. There will be one more saint for my Church.* I was astonished. Why would it be good if my sister were to die? Still, I was surrounded by a sense of deep spiritual peace. I did not understand what was happening to me. Could this be some sort of temptation? I wanted to see my confessor and tell him everything. Within moments, however, the doorbell rang and I received a telegram. My sister was dying and I had to leave for home immediately.

By the time I arrived in Tomsk Julia had already passed away. She had waited for me up to the last moment. Julia had been terribly proud of me and very happy that I would become a priest. I was told that before her death, my sister had prayed constantly. Our mother was with her when Julia had started to pray, "Hail, Mary . . ." but she lacked the strength to finish. In tears, Mama finished the prayer for her. Before she died, Julia said, "Mama, after my death, come to the church. We'll meet there." Our mother started to attend Mass and is now a member of the Church. Eventually, my father also was baptized in the Orthodox Church.

That same year, 1993, I professed my first vows, and so began a "honeymoon with the Lord." I needed no one and nothing other than Him. His love surrounded me. Were I in His place, I would have looked for someone better, but I was His choice, for which I am very grateful.

My studies in the seminary were easy and very pleasant. I was blessed with beautiful Claretian friends, who taught me the value of deep and close relationships, which were especially helpful on the path to my vocation. "A faithful friend is a sturdy shelter; he that has found one has found a treasure" (Sirach 6:14). One day I accompanied a friend to a meeting of the charismatic renewal. There, I spoke about spiritual life in Siberia and a bit about myself.

Following my talk, a gray-haired babushka threw herself at me and said, "Thank you, little grandson!" She explained that she had spent her childhood in Siberia and had experienced a number of difficult and painful situations. She said that the Lord had blessed her with spiritual gifts, yet something unexplainable blocked the development of her spiritual life. She wept all night after hearing my story and during that time the Lord revealed the answer to her. She had not been able to forgive the Russians for the wrong they had done to her family. Filled with resentment toward them, she could not even bear to listen to the Russian language. Having received this clarity, she resolved to forgive. She and I still share a deep relationship and I consider her my spiritual grandmother.

Countless times I have witnessed the Lord's reconciling and healing. It all begins with heartfelt forgiveness. There is no wrong that God cannot right.

GOLD TESTED IN THE FIRE

Jewish folk wisdom says, "The Most High, the All Powerful, before wounding a man prepares a bandage for him." The Lord placed many loving people in my life, who would pray that I might withstand the trials before me on my path to priesthood. Scripture reminds us:

> My son, if you come forward to serve the Lord, prepare yourself for temptation. Set your heart right and be steadfast, and do not be hasty in time of calamity. Cleave to him and do not depart, that you may be honored at the end of your life. Accept whatever is brought upon you, and in changes that humble you be patient. For gold is tested in the fire, and acceptable men in the furnace of humiliation. Trust in him, and he will help you: make your ways straight, and hope in him (Sirach 2:1-6).

In 1998, I began to prepare for final vows. At Mass each day I would offer up my vocation to the Lord, saying, "Not my will but Thine be done." In May of that year I began to have difficulty walking. A few months later, I was diagnosed with multiple sclerosis (MS). I accepted this finding with considerable calmness but the question emerged, "Lord, do you really want me to serve you?"

Lying in bed one morning, I stared at the ceiling. Knowing God was there, I chose to ignore Him. My inclination toward activity rebelled against the reality I faced—having an incurable disease that would eventually render me an invalid. I had dreamed of completing no less than two advanced degrees and accomplishing much on behalf of the Church, but all my plans appeared to be doomed. When I worked in the hospital with the sick, I used to speak about the salvific value of suffering and of offering sacrifices. Now it was time to apply this wisdom to myself, but I was not ready to do so. I resented God and, in mute protest, I refused to talk to Him. I had wasted so much time and energy on my vocation, and now this. I thought, *Where is your love in all this, Lord?*

I had kept my diagnosis a secret, yet one by one, people began to visit me, offering prayers and one simple message, "I love you." My visitors included religious brothers and lay friends, most of whom did not know each other but echoed the same message, increasing my amazement each time. After the ninth such declaration, I beseeched the Lord, "Was it you who sent these people? All right, let's talk. If you truly want me to serve you, bring it about that I am able to remain in my congregation. OK?" With that, the tension in my relationship with the Lord lessened, but it did not disappear altogether. (I only get into serious conflicts with those whom I truly love.)

The very next day, the housemaster came to see me. Having received word of my condition, he had called the provincial since such a serious disease could mean that I would have to leave the congregation. The provincial, in turn, sought counsel from the general superior. The reply from Fr. Aquilino Bocos Merino, CMF, would remain in my heart forever. He simply said, "He is a member of our family. In a family we do not abandon one another in times of difficulty. Let him stay." This was a true sign that the Lord wanted me to become a Claretian.

Various physical complications followed intense hormonal therapy. My brother Claretians remained steadfastly by my side the entire time like conduits for the Lord. Consequently, my relationship with the Lord matured. This was an amazing revelation of His love. I am eternally grateful for his constant presence during times of suffering when it appeared that He had abandoned me, but quite the opposite was true. The most important events along my spiritual path—baptism, first vows,

perpetual vows, ordination to the diaconate, and the priesthood—
have been accompanied by some form of suffering.

Following perpetual vows, I started to prepare for ordination
to the diaconate. Returning home on vacation, I talked with my
mother about my entire life. Seeing the results, I decided to try
to repair my relationship with my father. He and I agreed to meet
two days before my departure, a meeting with which I was very
pleased. But when I came home, I noticed that my mother was
very jealous, although she didn't speak to me about this. The
day before, she asked that I not meet with my father, but I had
already agreed. Despite my parents' divorce, I truly loved and
prayed for both of them. Desperately, I turned to Mother Mary
for help, and in time my mother sincerely repented of what she
had done. At my priestly ordination, my parents sat next to each
other. Alleluia!

A PRIEST FOREVER

The long-awaited day of my priestly ordination had finally
arrived. Transfiguration of the Lord Parish had been preparing
for this wonderful ceremony. Bishop Jerzy Mazur, SVD, who
had ordained me a deacon several months earlier, would also
ordain me a priest. Many parishioners attended and offered
their well wishes. They were thankful to God, my pastors,
and my parents. Witnessing this, I came to appreciate what a
privilege it was to pray, suffer, and fight for these very good and
accepting people.

Celebrating my first Mass and hearing my first confession
were truly unforgettable moments. I valued these two
sacraments because my intense spiritual growth began with
frequent confession and belief in the Real Preasence of
Christ in the Eucharist. Finally, after several years of priestly
ministry at Transfiguration parish, I was truly able to say that
I found home.

After a thorough check-up following my ordination, Russian physicians discarded the diagnosis of MS, but they were certain that I had another serious illness. All the while, my spiritual healing had been progressing. The Lord had healed so much in me that I was able to carry out my pastoral responsibilities with ease. From a human persepctive, I am wounded in many areas of my life, but it is precisely from this vulnerability that the strength comes to serve and to accept people as they are.

Jesus, the wounded healer, gives us sensitivity to others' problems and sufferings. I became sympathetic to the afflicted, especially those struggling with addiction and emotional problems. With the blessing of my pastor, Fr. Dariusz Bialek, and the assistance of Sr. Mary Katherine Malmros, SOLT, I founded a support group. From the outset, we placed our group under the patronage of St. Maximilian Maria Kolbe, patron saint of the addicted. While the group is based on the "Twelve-Step Program," we strive to focus on the meaning and role of spiritual growth and encourage participants to walk away from unmanageable situations.

With great joy, I also serve as spiritual director to the parish's pro-life and St. Vincent de Paul ministries. The Lord guides people very intensely. Observing this, I learn from them. Given the political and social environment of Russia, I strive to focus on deepening the spiritual life of our parishioners so that they in turn can "cast out into the deep." Through witness, those who do not know God may begin to ask questions about His existence.

Unfortunately, there is practically no advanced literature available in Russian on spiritual life and growth. Blessed by the help of Fr. Antonii, Sr. Mary Katherine, and her American friend Christina, we have begun to translate and publish such material. As will all my ministries, it is a project that is dear to my heart. My pastor, Fr. Dariusz, has been extremely supportive of my work.

Initially, when young men had approached me with questions about a priestly vocation (which is especially common during youth retreats), I soberly and rationally repeated, "Think it over, wait, it's not time yet." Later, I thought better of such advice. If a priest had spoken to me this way when I first sensed a call to the priesthood, how would it have affected my vocation? A vocation is not only a great gift but also a true mystery, something which proceeds from the depths of one's personal relationship with God. Much also depends, however, on those who help him accept this gift.

God chose me not because I have special qualities; rather in spite of my weaknesses and wounds. I gave nothing to God; it was He who gave me everything. He has made me a happy man because He has shown me that my life has value. I feel the presence and love of the Father. For every day I live in the state of grace, I give Him thanks. For every celebration of the sacrament of reconciliation and the Eucharist, I give Him thanks. For being able to function normally each day, I give Him thanks. For every second of prayer, every grain of love and gratitude, I give Him thanks. And for the miracle and unmerited gift of my vocation, I give Him thanks. I do not know if the Lord will find faith in me when He comes again, but I know I will have much for which to be thankful, especially for the unearned gift of priesthood.

&

2

THE HOLY SPIRIT'S "CHARLIE MCCARTHY"

FR. BENEDICT GROESCHEL, C.F.R.

As I climbed the fire escape to the fourth floor, I knew I was probably doing something wrong. My curiosity, though, got the better of me. When I got there, I stood on an overturned milk box and peeked in through the window. And there she was, the wicked witch, whom I recognized immediately from the first movie I had ever seen, *Snow White and the Seven Dwarfs*. I was frightened and jumped off the box, ran down the fire escape, and raced up the street to a place of refuge—the church. I knelt at the altar of the Blessed Virgin, whose blue votive lights I can still see in my memory. I prayed and prayed because I had seen *the witch*!

As I prayed, I wondered why the witch did not harm Sister Teresa Maria, the saintly sister who was in the elderly women's apartment bringing her food. It must have been because Sister was so good to her. Maybe if people were nicer to witches, I thought, they wouldn't be quite so bad.

As I knelt in the church sorting out this witch business, the words came to me as clear as a bell: "Be a priest." *A priest?* I was going to be fireman! As I left the church, I glanced over at the rectory, which looked a bit foreboding. God was calling me to be a priest. I was not enthused about the idea and told no one about the experience I'd just had.

In my life, and in the lives of many other people I have known, it is clear that our good Lord uses the unique experiences and circumstances of our lives to call to us. Such was the case here—God used the curiosity of a young boy to have him follow his second-grade teacher from Our Lady of Victory School in Jersey City, New Jersey, to learn more about the mission she was on. I had heard from the family barber, Giuseppe, that Sister Teresa Maria, the dedicated woman who taught seven-year olds for decades, took care of an old woman who was sick and lived on the fourth floor of his building. One day, I decided to follow sister as she carried a covered box or tray, from which steam escaped in the cold New York air. It was through this act of stealth that God spoke to me. How unique are the ways of the Lord.

My call to the priesthood was confirmed by another good nun, sparked this time by my father's curiosity. The year after the "witch incident" (may God bless that old woman, who was surely not a witch!), my new teacher, Sister Consolata, gave me a holy card on which she had written *ora pro me*. My father asked me to ask Sister why she wrote those words in Latin. "Because you are going to be a priest," was Sister's answer. From that moment to this, some sixty-five years later, I have never thought of being anything else.

It was the influence of the good Dominican sisters that introduced me to my vocation and to religious life. I admired the good work the sisters did. I was a friend of the "cook sisters," who worked in the kitchen. Their humility and simplicity impressed me greatly. I was educated by these sisters all through grammar school and high school, and I am, without a doubt, a "Sisters' Boy." With very few exceptions, the sisters I knew were extraordinarily fine Christians. Among the twenty truly outstanding human beings I have ever known, eleven of them were Catholic nuns, including Blessed Teresa of Calcutta and Mother Angelica of EWTN.

CHOOSING AN ORDER, LOVING THE POOR

Due to the early influence of the sisters in my life, I thought of becoming a religious order priest. I was much attracted to Saint Francis of Assisi. Though not a priest himself, this simple, humble friar loved and had the greatest devotion to the priesthood because of his love for the Blessed Sacrament. After looking at many orders, I settled on the Capuchin Franciscans, and in 1951, at the age of seventeen, I entered Saint Felix's Friary in Huntington, Indiana. There I met more very impressive people, one of whom was Father Solanus Casey, who was to become a venerable Servant of God.

For nine years I studied with the Capuchins to be a priest. While the actual seminary training was not difficult, the atmosphere before the Second Vatican Council was rather oppressive. I particularly lamented the lack of any apostolic work, but this was typical of seminaries for religious orders at that time. Fortunately, my superior, who understood what I needed, gave me work feeding the homeless men who came to the monastery every day. I did this for years. I also took care of the sick in the house.

One of the greatest blessings is that my seminary training was completely orthodox. Before Vatican II, there was not a great deal of emphasis on how to communicate the Gospel message to people, and the Catholic community was rather insulated from the rest of society. Except for the non-Christians at our foreign missions, we didn't think much about trying to convert people to the Catholic faith.

After my ordination in 1959, I was appointed chaplain of Children's Village, a psychiatric treatment center for emotionally-disturbed children located in Dobbs Ferry, New York. Those were fourteen of the happiest years of my life. I worked with an excellent staff and a fine program, which assisted children who had been badly scarred by their environment to make a good adjustment in life. Since leaving Children's Village more than thirty years ago, I have remained in contact with many of the boys who graduated from that institution. I have performed their weddings and baptized their children.

Not long after I was ordained, the winds of change blew through the Church in the form of the Second Vatican Council. No one was happier about this than I. I was particularly interested in ecumenism, and in the course of my life, I have preached in some two hundred Protestant churches and one hundred synagogues. In those days many people I knew were enthusiastic about ecumenism, and it was a great and joyous time in my life.

POST-VATICAN II CONCERNS

In the years following the Council, however, I became troubled by some directions the Church in the United States was taking. I was particularly concerned, for example, about the spread of confusing and false theological teachings regarding the mystery of the Incarnation and on issues of morality. While some of these teachings may not have been outright heretical, they were certainly inconsistent with the traditional doctrines of the Church.

Among these was a certain relativism in moral theology, which I found to be very dangerous. Then, too, there were certain skeptical approaches to teaching sacred Scripture, which seemed to undermine the very foundations of the Faith. The intellectual and scientific foundations of some of these theories were dubious at best and did not stand up to logic and investigation.

An additional concern of mine was the endless and unnecessary tinkering with the liturgy. I agreed that we needed to engage people much more in the liturgy than we had done when I was a boy. Before the Council, I had welcomed the beautiful new Easter Vigil liturgy, which had been revised by Pope Pius XII in the 1950s to allow for more general and convenient participation by the faithful. (Before Pope Pius' reform, the Vigil had been performed early on Holy Saturday morning before a congregation that, in most churches, consisted of a small number of mostly elderly people.) The liturgical changes which followed the Council, however, were of a very different nature. They seemed to turn the focus of worship away from praying to God toward entertaining the congregation. At the same time I was experiencing these concerns about a changing Catholic culture, I was pursuing a significant personal change as well.

In the 1960s, I began studying counseling and psychology, and I obtained a doctorate in counseling psychology from Columbia University in 1971. People often ask me if I had any trouble putting psychology together with my religious beliefs. The answer is no, not at all. The truths of the Catholic faith are like great stone mountains reaching up to the sky, and the theories of psychology are like snow on those mountains. They can make the mountains attractive but that's about all—and the snow doesn't last. As a matter of fact, many theories in psychology and psychotherapy that were most popular when I was a student—those based on Freud, Jung, Adler, Horney, Sullivan, and Rogers—have since fallen by the wayside. I was never tempted to examine the truths of faith from the viewpoint of psychology, although much of what I learned in psychology was helpful in a practical way.

In 1974, Terence Cardinal Cooke, the Archbishop of New York, asked me to open a retreat house and program for the spiritual growth of priests. This program of the Archdiocese of New York came to be called the Office for Spiritual Development. We also established a center for laypeople. It was with great sorrow that I left my full-time work with the poor at Children's Village, but I also believed that this new work had to be done as well. And, after all, the good cardinal was making this request. My work with priests was stimulating and challenging, but it did not, for the most part, bring me the same great joy I have experienced when working with the poor.

Work with the poor is, I believe, the most beautiful and, in many ways, the easiest work in the world. Long ago I read a quotation attributed to Saint Vincent de Paul, "Love the poor and your life will be filled with sunlight and you will not be frightened at the hour of death." Fortunately, I was able to continue part-time work with the poor, particularly with distributing food and arranging holiday celebrations, as well as keeping track of the many needy people I came to know through my work at Children's Village. Even today, I wonder whether that early experience with Sister Teresa Maria did not have an impact on me in this regard.

By the mid-1970s, it was obvious that many of the Church's institutions had been badly buffeted by the worldliness and cultural paganism that had engulfed the United States. As the media became an increasingly corrupt influence, as family life began to weaken, and as public immorality spread, it became clear that Catholic institutions were not up to the challenge. This was particularly noticeable in Catholic higher education and in the virtual collapse of many religious communities.

Now, at the beginning of the third millennium, many large religious communities in the United States face extinction. I see this as a terrible tragedy since I owe so much of my Christian life and formation to the sisters who taught me. My parents and grandparents always held religious sisters in the highest regard. I think they would all be greatly distressed to see the present confusion in the Catholic Church. Fortunately, the Lord took them before the chaos really spread.

TEACHING THE TRUTH...ON NATIONAL TV, OF ALL PLACES

For more than twenty years, I have been associated with EWTN, the television network established by Mother Angelica. Who would have thunk that a poor-ish kid from Brooklyn would have grown up to be a TV star. At this point in my life it is almost impossible for me to walk through an airport (and, in some cities, even down the street) without meeting people I do not know but who have become my friends through EWTN. I marvel at how God can use a poor schlep like myself to do a mighty work. (Be assured, this is not any unfounded self-deprecation. Until I get to heaven, I will certainly be a schlep, even if I do know a thing or two about theology and psychology). Whenever I speak or preach, I try to rely entirely on the Holy Spirit, so I cannot take credit for any of it. I feel very much like Charlie McCarthy, who was ventriloquist Edgar Bergen's dummy many years ago. The Lord simply speaks through me, once I get my ego out of the way.

This apostolate of television has afforded me an extraordinary opportunity to teach and defend the Catholic faith in this age of crisis. It is often said that those of us who profess to be evangelists for the Faith may never see the fruits of the seeds we sow. Though this has not been too important to me, I have been doubly blessed as a priest to see many of the fruits of these labors. The television outreach has provided a platform where literally hundreds of thousands of people hear my thoughts on weekly or month basis. A result of this has been thousands of letters of encouragement and affirmation over the years. What a gift to a priest this is. It makes me marvel all the more at the thousands of priests who faithfully live out their vocations in the quiet of their parishes, not receiving the plethora of "thank yous" I have been privileged to receive.

As I have mentioned, a great joy of mine has been to be able to defend the Catholic faith in this hostile age. Because of the efforts of EWTN and other evangelization and media apostolates, we have, to some degree, been able to stem the tide of secularism, humanism, and outright paganism that has overwhelmed so much of the culture in the past fifty years. As a priest and spiritual father, I have been able to live out the role of "protector," which is, I believe, written in the DNA of all men.

We priests are not just called to be healers and peacemakers, we are also called to be defenders—a calling that is sustained by God's grace.

In the past, some Catholics have taken a defensive attitude toward those who criticize the Church, as though we could never make a mistake. Although we should always be ready to give a reason for the hope that is in us (see 1 Peter 3:15), this posture of defensiveness is uncalled for—even silly—precisely because we should expect no less from the world (and even, alas, from some members of the Church). The apostles, on whom Christ founded the Church, abandoned Him on the very night that He instituted the Holy Eucharist at the Last Supper. Throughout the history of the Church, we see that the gates of hell have tried to prevail against her but have never succeeded. In the Church, past and present, you will find some of the very best human beings who have ever lived. Today, more than a billion people on earth profess faith in the Catholic Church. Statistically, when you get a bell curve of over a billion people, the ones at the top are going to be very good indeed—and the ones at the bottom are going to be truly awful.

JOHN PAUL THE GREAT AND BEGINNING A NEW COMMUNITY

In addition to my unexpected calling to the Catholic media, two of the greatest blessings in my priesthood are that I was able to witness the pontificate of Pope John Paul II and that I was able to found a religious order, which was also a calling I didn't pursue or expect.

I consider Pope John Paul II to be one of the ten outstanding popes in Church history. I have no doubt that history will give him the title "the Great," which in the past has been given only to pontiffs who have had a profound influence on the secular history of the world (such as St. Leo the Great, who sent Attila the Hun back from the gates of Rome). Some of the secular New

York newspapers actually suggested at the time of John Paul's 1979 visit that he would one day be called John Paul the Great.

In the last twenty-five years I have been guided and encouraged by the wonderful example of the late pope. John Paul II worked to restore devotion to Christ, especially in the Eucharist, to the Virgin Mary, and to the saints. He reached out to members of every religious denomination and nonetheless remained the most loyal defender of the Catholic faith. In season and out of season, he offered us a marvelous example, particularly in his old age and infirmity, as he traveled literally to the ends of the earth to proclaim the message of the Gospel.

John Paul II tried to restore to the Church something that had been lost in the confusion of the latter part of the twentieth century—namely, a sense of religious devotion. The psychological component of effective religion is religious devotion. It is a conviction that God in eternity knows me as an individual, that He cares about me, provides for me, hears my prayers, and expects things of me. When I fail, God expects me to repent, and when I close my eyes in death, I will meet Him.

Devotion to Jesus Christ, our divine Savior and Son of God, is especially important. Unfortunately, there has been a decline in religious devotion over the past forty years or so. Among Catholics there has been a decline in devotion to the presence of Christ in the Eucharist, devotion to His passion and death, and devotion to the Blessed Virgin Mary. As a psychologist with a religious background, I lament this tragic loss.

One of the most encouraging signs in recent times has been the coming of the new faithful. These are young people, who with no earthly explanation, are returning to an enthusiastic, orthodox, and devotional Catholicism. They have become an extremely important part of my life.

In 1987, as a result of the expressed need of some young friars, eight of us with great sadness left the Capuchin Franciscan order, despite our attempts to remain as a jurisdiction of that order. Through the sponsorship of John Cardinal O'Connor, Archbishop of New York, we were able to establish the Franciscan Friars of the Renewal. Soon after that we began a similar community of sisters. The purpose of the two communities is to work for the poor and to preach the restoration of the Catholic faith and life in every way possible. Our religious life is founded on prayer and devotion to the presence of Christ in the Eucharist, with a daily Eucharistic holy hour. Blessed Teresa of Calcutta and her Missionaries of Charity have profoundly influenced our attitudes toward our Franciscan vocation.

In nearly twenty years, our two communities have grown to a total membership of more than one hundred. The average age of our members is in the very early thirties. (If I dropped dead, it would be even lower, since I am by far the oldest member of the community.)

The Lord has blessed our work, not only in the slums of New York but also in the poorer sections of London and in an even more destitute area in Honduras. We have brothers and sisters from many countries, and I expect that the community will begin serving in some of these countries in the very near future. We probably have more people in training now than any other religious community in the United States. Even so, we are looking for more vocations because everywhere we go, people are clamoring for the preaching of authentic Catholicism and reform. The greatest blessing of our community is to provide shelter, care, and programs for the desperately poor. Laypeople and even other religious communities have generously responded to help us with this work.

The intention of our two communities is to live the spirit of the Franciscan order as defined by the Capuchin reform, which took place at the time of the Protestant Reformation. I do think that the Reformation era—when the Capuchins and Carmelites were reformed and the Jesuits were established—is not so different from our own. The brothers and sisters of our community are absolutely dedicated to preaching reform of the Church at the present time. The new faithful, the young people of our day, seem to be drawn to this reform with a powerful response. I only wish that we had more members to expand to other countries that are waiting for us to come. Our recent preaching tour of Ireland attracted thousands of people in a country where the Church has been shaken to its very foundation.

REFLECTIONS ON MY LIFE AS A PRIEST

As I look back over my life, I can see not only God's call but also the inspiration to follow that call. Many years ago as a teenager, I read about abandonment to Divine Providence and entrusting one's life completely to God. I made the consecration to the Sacred and Merciful Heart of Jesus when I was only sixteen, and I have tried to live by it. Despite my weaknesses and sinfulness, Christ has led me on and has always been there for me, even in the darkest moments. When I awoke one day in 2004 in the hospital, almost completely immobile after having been hit by a car, I learned that I had been medically dead with no signs of life for half an hour. I knew then that Providence was with me. The doctors called my survival a miracle, but I believe it was simply part of God's plan.

People often tell me that I have led a rather interesting life. There have been scary moments, such as when my brothers and I left our order to begin a new ministry, and there have been some dark times, especially when people I trusted failed the Gospel and were unable or willing to live up to it. But there have been an incredible number of joys. This is when we see the work of God—despite all human unworthiness—reaching down into souls often marred by sin, and bringing them to holiness and to a deeper knowledge of God and prayer. God is still running the world, despite the illusion that we are in charge.

Although I am old and looking forward to the next life—to the purification of my soul, which I know it so desperately needs, and finally to arriving at the divine kingdom—I sometimes wish I were younger so I could see the unfolding of the present drama. Although the Church has been humiliated, abused, and constantly attacked by the media, I think there will be a glorious flowering and second spring in the next fifty or sixty years. This is a time for renewal and reform. Those who open their hearts will lead challenging and fascinating lives; those who do not will be pulled into the morass of worldliness, overindulgence, and sinfulness which have become so characteristic of much of the public life and media of the United States and Europe.

If you read the history of the Church, you will see that it has gone through times like this before. It is in just such times that God calls generous souls to follow Him, to be the instruments of reform and renewal in the world. Perhaps He is calling you, in the circumstances of your life. In whatever vocation or state in life the Lord has called you, respond to His call and you will help renew the Church and the world.

And, please, *ora pro me* (pray for me)!

ə♦

3

A Life For and With the Poorest of the Poor

Fr. Sebastian Vazhakala, M.C.

"Sebastian," my father called to me in a grief-stricken voice one final time in the middle of the night. Then, as I approached his bedroom, he interrupted my labored footsteps with a despondent remark: "Bring a knife so you can finish killing your mother and me before you enter the seminary."

Although Thursday, July 20, 1962 was the longest and most tragic night of my life, it was equally as agonizing for my dearly beloved parents. None of us slept. Each hour, my father called me into his room to ask if my decision had changed. All the while, my poor mother lay weeping into her pillow. I had nothing to say as I had no intention of changing my plans, and words would simply not comfort them. They had thought that I would live with them forever and could not bear to imagine a life in which we would see each other only infrequently. I knew they loved me immensely, and it was out of love that my father did everything possible to block the road to my vocation to priesthood.

The lights that had illumined my rough path were out and I was faced with uncertainty. *Should I abandon my desire to become a priest?* The night was long and the road was dark. I don't know how or from where I received the courage and grace to overcome my obstacles, but I decided to walk forward in blind faith.

I had always felt undeserving of my father's extraordinary love for me. On my way to check my exam results at the end of my junior year in high school he said, "If you fail, then you will not continue with your studies." My family faced an enormous trial that year, 1961. An accidental fire turned our house into a pile of ash and left us with a mound of debt. Upon our return from Saturday Mass and Marian devotions that day, April 29, my brother and I found our house in ruins. Shocked and trembling, we cried out loud. Our fear turned to panic, however, when we thought that we had lost our youngest sister, Leelamma, who was only two years old at the time. Providentially, neighbors had taken her to their home.

Ironically, our devotions earlier that day had included a novena to Our Lady of Perpetual Help. Confronted by the arduous task of rebuilding the house ourselves, we relied on divine intervention. Like Our Lady, my mother had encouraged us to rely on God and pray continually, so we doubled our family prayer time and trusted that God would not abandon us. He did not.

My name was listed among the students being promoted to the final year of high school. I knew that keeping his promise to allow me to complete my studies meant more hardship for my father and our family, as the tuition expense would increase our debts. Seemingly impossible circumstances would befall my every step, but each time the Lord led me on. Boarding was my next hurdle. The school's headmaster advised me to find housing closer to school, since walking four miles each way took up valuable study time and I needed to prepare for the final government exams. After completing my studies and passing the exams, I took a job at a small bank near my home. This pleased my father but I was unhappy.

My call to the priesthood became clear to me in April 1962, while I attended a vocation retreat in a small town in the district of Kannur in my home state of Kerala. The famous spiritual director Msgr. Mathew Mankuzhikary led our retreat, and many of the prayers he taught and points he stressed remain with me to this day. A reading from the autobiography of St. Thérèse of Lisieux also made a lasting impression. In it, she describes the tremendous hardship she went through to enter Carmel at the age of fifteen. "If necessary," she began one passage, "I would go to Rome to speak with the pope [for permission]." She eventually resorted to doing so.

By the end of the retreat, there was no doubt in my mind that Jesus wanted me to be a holy priest. I desired to be a missionary, but I knew that type of commitment would completely devastate my parents. Instead, I decided to pursue ordination for our diocese, Tellicherry. The procedure to enter into the diocesan seminary was not complicated. I filled out the necessary application, easily passed the written and oral exams, and had no trouble relating my vocational yearning in an interview. But I ran into a problem when it came time for my father to complete and sign the permission form. To my father, my desire to enter the seminary and leave home was a personal affront. He felt as though I was ungrateful and was rejecting the love and devotion he and my mother had poured on me over the years.

Night after night, I got down on my knees and prayed. Heaven, it seemed, remained silent to my cries. Then, out of the blue, came news that I had won the diocesan catechism prize. Bishop Sebastian Valloppilly requested that I claim my award personally. He was glad to see me, but I was happier to be in *his* presence. I explained my longing for a priestly vocation, but he said that he could not accept me without my father's permission. He suggested that I return home and work for one year as he had done when he was young. After that, he would reconsider. Handing me his personal rosary and a lovely autographed spiritual book, he sent me away.

I returned home, half filled with joy and half with sadness. Eager to know what was going on, my father was relieved to hear the bishop's recommendation for me. I was disappointed to learn that my father had secretly appealed to the bishop, saying he could not bear losing me and that he needed me at home. Despite my father's efforts, a week later I received an invitation to join the new group of seminarians who had already begun their studies. Bishop Valloppilly had changed his mind. "Come immediately to the seminary," he wrote.

It is not always easy or simple to discern and carry out the will of God. Sometimes, it appears humanly impossible. Consider Our Lady's unconditional response to God's will. It brought terrible pain, confusion, and sorrow in the life of St. Joseph, even though he too was intent on doing God's will.

As priests, we are tried in the crucible of intense suffering in order to be purified and make our vocation stronger. Jesus wants us to build our vocation not on the sand of apparent glamour and excitement, but on the rock of trials and hardships. He knows that sooner or later the wind will blow, the rain will fall, the food will come, and the house will be buffeted. However, it will not fall if it is built on solid rock (see Matthew 7:24-27).

THE FOUNDATION THAT WAS LAID FOR ME

Jesus, how much you have suffered for me, let me offer this pain in union with your suffering. My mother taught my siblings and me to say this prayer any time we were in pain—serious or minor.

It is said that a majority of vocations are forged through a family life rich in faith. To say my faith formation was rich would be a significant understatement. My parents and grandparents were committed Catholics, and our home was my first school. It was there that my sisters, brothers, and I learned to pray. As a family, we prayed on our knees with arms outstretched for the Rosary for at least an hour every night. A Scripture reading, the litany of Our Lady, and devotional songs followed our prayer hour. We also had novenas and devotional readings. The holy seasons of Advent and Lent were observed strictly in our home. Throughout the year, we also observed the months that bore devotion on the traditional Catholic calendar. January was dedicated to St. Sebastian, March to St. Joseph, May to Our Lady, June to the Sacred Heart, and November to the faithful departed. Prayer and sacrifice were routine in our home, and we were reared on both from a very young age. Leading by example, my parents invited a poor family to our home for a meal each Wednesday. They also took the initiative to organize family prayer groups.

Lessons on the doctrines of the Faith were regular and very serious throughout the Kerala diocese. The Sunday children's Mass was followed by two hours of catechism instruction. Children from ages five to about twenty were separated according to grade level and were given a course syllabus and textbooks. Exams were part of the curriculum, and we were awarded prizes for good grades. The prizes often included biographies of the saints, which spurred in me a desire to become a saint. My thoughts about sainthood predated any aspirations of priesthood. Later, the two desires would go hand in hand, although only the latter is being realized and the former is still pending.

In addition to a great devotion to the faith, punctuality was another priority in our home. My parents taught us that it was part of being respectful. If by chance we were late for anything, we had to apologize and then offer an explanation. Gradually over the years, my father mellowed and became less strict and severe. By comparison, the younger children in our family were rather spoiled by my parents, but they did have their older siblings to guide them and we delighted in the opportunity.

I was four- or five-years-old when I first longed to be like one of the martyrs my mother read about like St. Sebastian or St. George. I never imagined that one day I would actually see the historic places of so many martyrs and confessors whose lives I experienced through books. I am in awe of the tremendous blessings God has bestowed upon me during my life, yet I feel as though I am not grateful enough. As St. Paul once said, "I am what I am by the grace of God." I also echo the sentiments of Blessed Teresa of Calcutta, "Jesus, my own Jesus. I am weak, sinful and unworthy." To this I would add, "I am miserable" because Blessed Teresa asked Jesus to look for a more worthy and holier person than herself, but I did not do that. As St. Matthew did upon hearing Jesus' words, "Follow me," I simply got up and followed Him.

THE DECISION TO GO

The clock struck four times as I got up and prepared to go to St. Mary's Church in Edoor the morning after the all-night ordeal with my parents. In order to be there by 6:00 a.m., I had to begin my seven-mile hike in the dark. The pre-dawn sky paled in comparison to the darkness that lay within me. The parish priest, Fr. Matthew Moongamackel, was in the confessional when I arrived. I knew him well, and following penance and Mass, he invited me to breakfast. There, he gave me twenty-five rupees for my journey to the seminary. I thanked him and thanked God for him. I returned home and met the parish priest, who had only been there a few months. I mentioned my financial dilemma but he did not respond. The Lord knew what I needed most. This parish priest gave me a short biography of St. John Berchmans. It later became a helpful tool in observing the rules and other religious and spiritual practices, especially the practice of charity in the community. St. Berchmans said, "Community life is one of the greatest penances for me."

Perched like a lion, my father sat motionless as I approached the house around noon that day. We did not exchange words. He was furious. As I packed my bags for the seminary, I heard my mother say, "Anyway, he has decided to go. Please accompany him." Much to my surprise, he did. Together we went to see Bishop Valloppilly. After greeting us, the bishop turned to my father and said, "It was due to his prayers that he was accepted. Now go to the seminary and meet the rector. He knows everything." So off we went. The rector spoke to me in English, and I could hardly understand him, as my native language is Malayalam.

Classes had begun on July 3rd and it was already the 21st. The seminarians were busy decorating the place for a visit the following day by the apostolic nuncio, Archbishop James Knox. They told me he would celebrate Mass and then he and Bishop Valloppilly would stay for breakfast and a group photo.

That day, my father took me into town and bought me everything I needed, from plates and cutlery to cloth for my shirts. Seminarians wore white shirts, and since I had none, I borrowed one from a classmate until I was able to sew my own. By the time we were through shopping, the buses had stopped running for the day. My father was not permitted to spend the night in the seminary nor could he make the thirty-mile trip back home, so he rented a room in town and reached home the following day. I was humbled. My father, who had been so adamantly opposed to me entering the seminary, was making more sacrifices for me. Feeling sad and guilty, I thought all night about my beloved parents to whom I must have looked so cruel, so unkind and unbending.

THE GIFT AND MYSTERY OF THE PRIESTHOOD

As part of the golden jubilee of his ordination, Pope John Paul II published an account of his priesthood entitled *Gift and Mystery*. How true it is that the priesthood is, and will always be, a great gift and an unfathomable mystery. I venture to add that for a person like me—so weak, sinful, and unworthy—it is the gift of all gifts one can receive in this world.

The Lord is truly amazing, for another great gift has been my vocation to serve the poorest of the poor with Blessed Teresa of Calcutta in the family of the Missionaries of Charity. My desire to become a missionary was fulfilled after all. Working with Blessed Teresa for three decades, I was one with the poor as well as one of them.

On the eve of Mission Sunday 1971, I was ordained a priest in the city of Calcutta. The Gospel that had been chosen for the ordination Mass read, "The Spirit of the Lord is upon me, because he has anointed me to preach good news to the poor. He has sent me to proclaim release to the captives and recovering of sight to the blind, to set at liberty those who are oppressed, to proclaim the acceptable year of Lord" (Luke 4:18-19, from Isaiah 61:1-2).

I had been a professed brother of the Missionaries of Charity by the time of my ordination, and even during my theological studies at the papal Athaeneum in Pune, India. Yet, I still needed time to understand the breadth and length, the height and depth of that passage of the Gospel. And, I must confess, I have yet to fully grasp or live it in all its fullness. I feel that each day I begin all over again. Each day is a new day, which offers new and better possibilities to recognize, love, and serve the Lord through my brothers and in the distressing disguise of the poorest of the poor.

My first meeting with Blessed Teresa was on November 30, 1966, in the motherhouse parlor in Calcutta. One of the first things Mother said to me was that the work she and her sisters were doing was not social or philanthropic work but God's work. That meant that the Spirit of the Lord was upon her—that He had anointed her. He had called and chosen her to work with and for the poor, the sick, the dying, the lepers, and, later, those with AIDS. He had chosen her to visit the prisoners and befriend them, to cure the sick of their illnesses, both of body and soul.

Mother would reveal a special insight that likely came from some sort of intense communion with the Lord. In a 1947 letter to Archbishop F. Perier, S.J., she wrote: "There are plenty of nuns to look after the rich and well-to-do people, but for my very poor, there are absolutely none. For them I long, for them I love—wilt thou refuse?"

Clearly, these are the words of our Lord Jesus. In the same letter, she revealed that Jesus wanted her to carry Him and to be His light:

> My little one, come, come, carry me into the holes of the poor —Come, be My light—I cannot go alone—They don't know Me—you come—go amongst them—carry Me with you into them—how I long to enter their holes—their dark, unhappy homes. Come, be their victim—in your immolation, in your love for Me, they will see Me, know Me, want Me—Offer more sacrifices—smile more tenderly, pray more fervently and all the difficulties will disappear.

How can anyone ignore or refuse such a heartbreaking plea of Jesus? How can anyone fail to see the hovels of the poor? And how could Blessed Teresa ever consider the life she was living and the work she was doing *her* work and not our Lord's? Truly the work of the Missionaries of Charity is God's work; therefore, it must be done with great love and devotion. How can I, a mere human being, feel worthy of such a noble vocation? Blessed Teresa also felt weak, sinful, and unworthy, but Jesus came forward and told her: "You are, I know, the most incapable person, weak and sinful, but just because you are that, I want to use you for my glory. Wilt thou refuse?"

These are God's words. He chooses the weak, the sinful, and the unworthy for His glory. This is why He has also chosen me. Still, we recite each day, especially after Holy Communion, the prayer attributed to Pope Paul VI: "Make us worthy, Lord, to serve our fellow men throughout the world, who live and die in poverty and hunger. Give them, through our hands, this day their daily bread, and by our understanding love, give peace and joy."

My vocation to the priesthood in the Missionaries of Charity is nothing less than a sheer gift from God, yet I continue to feel unworthy, often asking, *Lord, why me. Why not someone more worthy? Look at the hundreds of holy, intelligent, and gifted people who could serve you much better than I. I do not understand your designs and ways.* It is written, however, "For who has known the mind of the Lord, or who has been his counselor? For from him and through him and to him are all things" (Romans 11: 34, 36).

Blessed Teresa often instructed us saying, "Accept whatever he gives and give whatever he takes with a big smile." Whatever He gives us is not only good for us but also *the best* for us. We read in Scripture, "If you then, who are evil, know how to give good gifts to your children, how much more will your Father who is in heaven give good things to those who ask him" (Matthew 7:11). Still, it seems impossible to proceed sometimes. During these crossroads, we receive help from above in very unexpected and unusual ways.

The spiritual combat will continue, but so too will the Divine help to fight the good fight, to run the race, to grow in faith, to die of love, and to die for love. Love will remain unconquered— conquering everything and everyone. With time, everything will disappear from the face of the earth, but not love. Men and women will die today or tomorrow and someday so shall you and I, but our deeds of love will never die. This is all that matters. I want to become a slave to the invincible Love, in full freedom and clear knowledge.

BECAUSE OF GOD'S MERCY

Today I am a priest of God because of His mercy, but my priesthood must bloom in the fertile soil of love. In me and around me there should not be anything but love. My priestly life and ministry must be nothing but the fruit of my intimate and uninterrupted union with the source and fountain of this enduring love, the holy and most undivided Trinity—Father, Son and Holy Spirit.

My priesthood bloomed and continues to blossom in the soil and in the midst of a unique group of people, whom I consider very specially loved by God. They are the poorest of the poor, the weakest of the weak, the less than the least of all. I, too, am one like and one of them, who was ordained to minister and to serve and guide them to God.

Regarding priestly vocations, Dominican Father Jean-Baptiste Lacordaire (1802-1861) wisely and insightfully wrote:

> To live in the midst of the world,
> Without wishing its pleasures;
> To be a member of each family,
> Yet belonging to none;
> To announce the good news to the poor,
> To heal the broken hearted,
> To share all their sufferings;
> To penetrate all secrets;
> To go from men to God
> And offer him their prayers
> To return from God to men
>
> To bring pardon and hope;
> To have a heart of fire for charity
> And a heart of bronze for chastity;
> To teach and to pardon,
> Console and bless always.
> What a glorious life! And it is yours,
> O priest of Jesus Christ!

A PRIEST—TODAY, TOMORROW, FOREVER.

On the day of my priestly ordination Mother Teresa penned a note on the back of a photograph of herself and sent it to me along with a letter apologizing for being unable to attend the ceremony.

My dear Brother Sebastian, . . . It is painful for me not to be
present at your first sacrifice–but you know through this my

sacrifice, I will be close to you. My prayers will be with you...
His chosen one.

The only one who brings Christ on the altar.
The only one who can say,
'This is my body, This is my blood'
And you, my brother, are His priest.

God bless you,
Mother
23.10.1971

I pray that God will continue to guide my heart and my
vocation. May His mercy and grace be with all who struggle to
discern His calling. God bless you.

ॐ

Editors' Note: *Fr. Sebastian Vazhakala, M.C., along with Blessed Teresa
of Calcutta, co-founded the Missionary of Charities–Contemplative, a
community of priests and brothers. Fr. Vazhakala was born in Kerala, India
on September 2, 1942, and he was baptized in his family's parish church,
St. Mary's, which was founded in A.D 105 in what is now Kuravilangad,
Kottayam, Dt. Kerala on the Southwest tip of India. His Roman Catholic
background descends from the Syro Malabar Rite whose origins date back to
A.D. 52 when St. Thomas the Apostle was in India.*

4

"FOR ME TODAY, YOU ARE JESUS CHRIST"

FR. KEVIN SCALLON, C.M.

During World War II, the Manor House Hotel on the shores of Lough Erne, Northern Ireland, served as a residence for American army officers. Not long ago, I had dinner with my older brother at the hotel, where he told me of the building's history. His words took me back to my earliest days at our Irish parish church. I can still see the GIs lining up outside the church on Sunday morning and marching in to the front pews reserved for them. I have often wondered since then how many of those young men landed and died on the beaches of Normandy.

I was a child during that war, having been born into a large Irish family. We lived on a farm, and even during the war when there was a great scarcity of everything, we always seemed to have plenty to eat and acres of space to roam and play.

Our pastor—affectionately known by his fellow priests as "Chicago Jack"—was a distinguished old man who had spent many of his early years of the priesthood in the United States. I remember whenever he spoke about the love of the Sacred Heart, his voice would crack and he would stop. I used to wonder why he did that. Later on, I found out that he was deeply moved in the Spirit by the thought of the love of Christ for us.

My father and mother had a great love for priests and often invited them to our home. I can recall one of the chaplains from a nearby U.S. army camp coming to dinner and my being intrigued by his American accent and his rimless glasses. My father had

47

a boyhood friend who became a Passionist priest, so many Passionists and other priests visited our home over the years. My earliest memories of priesthood were warm and very positive, and had a deep influence on my life.

My family lived in an atmosphere of prayer. We would pray the Rosary together as a family, and I would see my mother constantly fingering her beads and my father reading his prayer book. On First Fridays, we would pile into the car and drive off to confession at the Passionist monastery. When you see your father and your mother leading you in prayer, observe them going regularly to confession, and witness their love for the Eucharist and their fidelity in attending Mass, you do not need many sermons to convince you of the importance of these things. Faith, prayer, and sacramental living were in the very air we breathed.

It was not just the influence of my parents that I imbibed, but also the witness of my older brothers and sisters who, when I think of it now, lived exemplary lives as young men and women. In this atmosphere, my vocation took root. It was around the time of my first Holy Communion that I began to sense a real call to become a priest. I can say now that the Eucharist had a special and profound meaning in my life. I felt drawn to it; to Christ whom I believed was present there.

My parents sent all of us to boarding schools for our high school education. In God's providence, they sent me to a school run by the Vincentian Fathers. The Vincentians who taught me were real men of God, dedicated to their work, and clearly at home with their priestly ministry. It was here that my priestly vocation really became clear to me, at a particular moment one day during the sacrament of Reconciliation. Until then, my experience of going to confession was not always happy, especially during the week of the parish missions which we had every year. Some crusty old missionaries were convinced that at ten or eleven years of age I had made a bad start in life and needed severe admonition, which they fearlessly delivered. So when I went to the Vincentian, Father Hugh, it was as if I had come into the presence of Jesus himself; so gentle and Christ-like was he. I had never met anyone who so reflected the loving kindness of Christ as this good priest.

MEETING CHRIST HIMSELF

An incident occurred during those years which I still recall as having a certain mystical influence on me. On one of our many compulsory walks, I saw a poor man to whom my attention was drawn in a strange way. I can remember looking at him and seeing him look back at me. At the time, I was puzzled by the encounter, but I later became convinced that somehow I had met Christ himself. From that moment on, the call to a priestly vocation seemed to crystallize in my thinking. Over the period of my boyhood I had considered many careers. I fancied myself as a pilot, an architect, a great singer, and so on. These would soon pale compared to the force that was now drawing me in the direction of the priesthood.

A vocation is also a deeply personal thing, a unique mystery of God's grace. I have often wondered why, out of all of my brothers, the Lord chose *me* to be a priest. There is something about the way that God draws one to the priesthood that puts everything else in second place. A young man considers the possibility of a priestly vocation at an age when his thoughts turn very much in the direction of young women. Yet, somehow he knows that the price to be paid, especially celibacy, is little compared to the prize that is the priesthood. Youth is the time when people choose to do great things. I saw the priesthood as the greatest of all.

An Irish actor named Ray McAnalley, who had once studied for the priesthood, gave a very good description of what a vocation is: "A vocation is where you begin to suspect that you are about to be called." You go to the seminary with this strong suspicion and, after a year or two, you begin to realize that this is either for you or not for you. In Ireland in those days there was not a great deal of talk about celibacy. It was one of those things that was taken for granted if you wanted to become a priest.

Even at the age of eighteen when I entered the seminary, I knew that leaving girls behind was going to be a big sacrifice. Sexual attraction is a powerful human emotion—you do not need long lectures from learned people to understand what you are giving up. And if chaste living and virginity is a good preparation for Christian marriage, how much better is it for those preparing for a life of celibacy? I become a little impatient with those who would have us believe that for a man to be successful in the celibate life, he needs to have had mature sexual relationships. Sexual experience outside of marriage fosters great immaturity in the lives of many, to say nothing of its impact on the priesthood and the Church at large.

After having received so much from the Vincentians, I was received into their community on October 7, 1953, the Feast of the Holy Rosary. My first year was one of spiritual formation in which we were steeped in the life and lore of St. Vincent de Paul, learning the rich ways of the order he founded. Our seminary life was also robustly masculine. We had plenty of Gaelic football, rugby, and soccer. On the seminary farm, we looked after pigs, poultry, and cattle. We milked cows, fed chickens, and lived a Spartan existence of prayer, study, work, and asceticism. The priest who was in charge of our formation had been educated by the Trappists, and much of what influenced him in his youth he passed on to us. At all times, we were on our honor to behave and had no deans monitoring our conduct. All in all, in those pre-Vatican II times, we received a well-rounded college-level and theological education.

There were some features of our Vincentian life which were derived from the order's "French connection." For example, we were not allowed to vacation with our families. Our time off was spent at one of the Vincentian high schools in Dublin. We were not permitted either to read the daily newspapers or go to movies (there was virtually no television in Ireland in the 1950s). This detachment from family and from the outside world meant that we led something of a monastic existence. This kind of detachment can bear fruit in the spiritual life, but I found that it has its limitations and may not have been the best preparation for a busy pastoral ministry.

In due course, after eight years of study, seven classmates and I were ordained to the priesthood at Holy Cross College in Dublin on May 27, 1961. The ceremony—to put it mildly— was not an impressive liturgical event. We were told to show up that morning in plenty of time for the 8:30 Mass, which would be presided over by John Charles McQuaid, Archbishop of Dublin. Archbishop McQuaid was a man of extreme liturgical and ritual propriety. When he ordained you to the priesthood, you *knew* that you were a priest forever according to the order of Melchizedek. Apart from what was in the rite of ordination, no other words were spoken. Afterwards, we were treated to a breakfast of warm tea and cold boiled eggs in the seminary dining room. Then we met our parents and family members to impart our first priestly blessing.

TO ENGLAND AND AFRICA

To finally be a priest was incredible and wonderful—like a dream come true. I felt different. I knew that the sacrament of Holy Orders, the laying on of hands and the prayer of the Church, had forever changed me.

After my ordination, I was appointed as an assistant pastor in a Vincentian parish in Sheffield, England, where my order had worked for more than one hundred years. I arrived in early October 1961.

While I was not familiar with the term "culture shock" that is exactly what I experienced. Sheffield was a heavily industrialized steel town—a metropolis compared to the sheltered existence I had lived in for the previous four years. Imagine being lifted from

the gentle, rolling country hills of County Wicklow and being
put down in the "dark satanic mills" of the industrial north of
England where you could eat the air pollution with a spoon. One
of my confreres wryly remarked, "Wouldn't it be awful to live in
Sheffield all your life and then go to hell when you die?" At the
time, the city was going through extensive urban renewal. The
narrow streets and housing of the Industrial Revolution were
being swept away, only to be replaced by even more hideous high-
rise flats.

It was into this social and demographic upheaval that I was
launched into pastoral ministry. One of my responsibilities was
serving as chaplain to a large hospital. My abiding memory of
that place was assisting a man at the moment of death as Elvis'
"Viva Las Vegas" blared from a radio at the other end of the
ward. I remember thinking, "Lord, when I go, please let it be an
operatic tenor and not Elvis who serenades me to the gates of
paradise."

The upside to all of this was the people of Yorkshire
themselves. They loved the priests and had a tremendous sense
of loyalty to their parish. They were a warm-hearted, good-
humored people who lived hard lives working in the steelworks
and the coal mines. I made friendships there which have lasted
to this day.

My pastor there was a wise man who was well aware of
my naiveté and youthful inexperience. He taught me many
pastoral skills and ways of dealing with people which helped
me enormously. He used to say, "Don't imitate me; always be
yourself. If you do that, you will be a successful pastor." After
more than forty-five years as a priest, I can bear witness to these
sage words: do not try to be someone else. Be yourself—or the
people will see right through you.

To escape the air pollution of the city, I would get into my
Volkswagen and drive out onto the Yorkshire Moors and walk
there for an hour or two before returning to the parish. During

these long walks, it became very clear to me was that most of what I learned in the seminary, while being good in itself from a theological point of view, was not of much practical use when it came to preaching. At that time, preaching and homiletics were at an all-time low in the Church. The study of Scripture and homiletics, which should have been given priority in our academic program, almost got squeezed out. This resulted in an impoverished style of preaching which everyone found unsatisfactory, especially the people who had to listen to us!

During my second year at Sheffield, Pope John XXIII opened the Second Vatican Council and I can recall how excited I felt when I first heard the news. I remember at Mass one Sunday telling the people about the Council and uttering a little prophecy, stating that I thought the Church would never be the same again. With the coming of Vatican II and the issuing of its successive documents, I felt very much that the Holy Spirit was beginning a great work in the Church and in the world. I recall reading the first document, *Sacrosanctum Concilium*, on the liturgy. I thought it was so beautiful and such a revelation, so anointed by the Holy Spirit and so true. After that, I could not wait for each of the Council documents to be issued, and I devoured them when they came. I can recall thanking God that I was living my priesthood at this moment in the history of the Church and witnessing things coming to pass that so many had hoped for.

After three years in Sheffield, I received a letter from my provincial expressing his delight and confidence in me personally and telling me that he was appointing me to our small mission band in Nigeria, in West Africa. I was to take up my post in October of 1964. Well, if I thought I experienced culture shock in Sheffield, it was nothing to compare to the jolt I experienced in tropical southern Nigeria, surrounded by palm trees, rain forests, and high humidity. Yes, air conditioning had been invented by then, but it certainly had not arrived at our mission in Ikot Ekpene.

My first experience was language school in a place which was quite a distance from our mission. During my studies I came down with my first bout of malaria. It was a severe fever and took a great deal out of me at the time. I went through a bit of a dark night of the soul and felt very sorry for myself. This dark night had nothing to do with my priesthood—which I loved and never questioned— but had everything to do with the experience of being sick with malaria in a strange place and in a very alien climate. Malaria has a depressing effect on people. But my despondency passed and, after I recovered physically and began my work of giving retreats, my spirits lifted. My few years in Africa were perfectly wonderful in terms of being a priest. I was in a place where there was none of the hide-bound clericalism that governed life back home. There was a camaraderie and brotherhood among all of us who ministered there. In those days in Nigeria, the vast majority of people were poor. I came to understand why the poor bless us with the privilege of ministering to them. It was only when the Lord allowed me to see himself in them and to see him in my priestly ministry that I understood what a blessing it is to be called to help the poor. One who doesn't see Christ in the poor will be unable to help them. Movie stars and rock stars can generate publicity about the plight of the poor, but even for them the path towards helping the afflicted passes through the heart of Christ. The poor are Christ.

TWO LESSONS IN LOVE

During this time, Nigeria was experiencing a lot of political upheaval which ultimately ended in civil war and the declaration of the Republic of Biafra. The war of independence that ensued was mostly one of attrition. The federal government blockaded the Biafrans into their own small area and proceeded to starve them into submission. The government would not let them secede was because the Biafran area contained vast resources of oil.

Some of my most formative experiences as a priest happened to me during this time. I was appointed pastor of a parish in the heart of Ibo-land. As well as ministering to the local people, I had to care for thousands of refugees who were pouring in from the south. Because of the federal army's blockade, the only food and supplies that were getting through were those being flown in illegally to an airport in San Thome. The material was distributed to each parish and then given to the poor by priests or lay leaders. Of course, there was never enough of anything.

Perhaps the greatest lesson I ever learned about being a priest came from the most unlikely of teachers. It happened one Sunday after I had returned from saying several Masses around my parish. I came back to my mission house expecting it to be surrounded, as was often the case, with dozens of starving people looking for food. As it happened, there was no one there. I was relieved, thinking I would go inside and have my breakfast of boiled eggs, toast, and instant coffee.

Just as I was heading in, a young woman who was leaning heavily on a staff came around the house. She looked at me and said, "Good morning, Father." I replied irritably, "What do you want?" She smiled and repeated, "Good morning, Father." I said, "Good morning. What do you want?" She said, "Please, Father, let me tell you my story." I groaned inwardly because I had heard so many stories and really was not in the mood for yet another one. But I said to her, "Please, tell me your story."

She began to tell me how she was driven from her home many kilometers south of where she was now. She, her husband, and their four children had been forced to leave because of the retreating armies. She recounted how, on the way, her little family had died of hepatitis. I was inclined to believe her, knowing how many people at that time were succumbing to this disease. (The wonder was that we did not all die of it.) She said "Please, Father, give me something to keep my body and soul together until this war is over."

I asked one of the parish's native catechists to bring her some food, clothing, a blanket, and other items, including salt (a vital commodity in very short supply). After the catechist handed them to her, she set it all down on the ground and began to sing and dance around it in a circle. Still thinking of my eggs and coffee, I asked the catechist what on earth she was doing. He said, "Oh, Father, she is thanking God for you."

By now, the sun was high in the sky and it was very hot, so I went over to her and said, "So you believe in God, do you?" She looked at me with a kind of astonished disbelief and said, "Yes, Father, I believe in God." I think she had it on the tip of her tongue to ask me, "Do *you* believe in God?", but being a good charitable woman, she refrained. I then asked her, "Do you believe in Jesus Christ?" To this she made no reply, but she went over and picked up the things we had given to her and gathering them in her frail arms, she came and stood directly in front of me. She said, "Father, you are asking me whether I believe in Jesus Christ. For me today, *you are Jesus Christ.*"

Her words hit me like a thunderbolt. The truth of it pierced my heart and I felt chastised and blessed at the same moment. In one sentence she had summed up for me the essence of what it means to be a priest without my making the slightest attempt to be Christ-like to her. I sometimes wonder if God sends angels to us priests in the form of poor people to remind us of the really important things in life. Her words have lodged in my heart all of these years and have provided me with powerful inspiration in the midst of all the controversies, changes, and scandals that have beset the priesthood.

Another lesson I learned at that time was in relation to the holy Eucharist. The very first morning after I arrived in my parish, a man came to my door and asked me to follow him to his village because an old man was dying there. When I arrived, I went in and found the man curled around a pungent, smoky fire in his little mud house. He said, "You know, Father, there has been no priest in this parish for over three years now. I prayed that you would come. I prayed every day to St. Joseph that I would not die without seeing a priest." He paused for a moment and then continued. "My own name is Joseph and I am so glad that you have come because today I am going to die."

I was deeply moved by the simple faith of this old man. After I had ministered to him all the comfort that the Church brings to dying people through the sacraments and the apostolic blessing, he looked up at me with a beautiful smile on his face and breathed his last.

When I came out from his house I was met by two hundred or so villagers, and their appearance shocked me. They were dressed in filthy rags and were severely emaciated. Most were covered with awful suppurating sores. The man who had brought me said, "Father, let me tell you about this village. The government rounded up all the lepers in this area and told us to come and live here. They said that they would send us food and medicine, but they have never sent us anything."

I asked, "So you are all suffering from leprosy are you?" He answered, "All of us, even the children."

I was so moved with pity for them that I promised I would return in a few hours to help them. Back at my mission, I loaded up my old Volkswagen car with all the food, medicine, bandages, blankets, and clothing that I could find and drove back to the village. There I was met by the leader of the village. He received all that I offered with disinterested detachment. My pride was hurt and I thought, "Even St. Vincent, on one of his better days, did not do as well as I have done today and these people did not even thank me." Such was my vanity and egotism. I have learned since that it is I who should have been thanking them for the privilege of ministering to Christ in their midst.

I asked the leader if he would like me to come and say Mass in their village. Again, reflecting the deep depression that was in the heart of everyone there, he said "Oh, all right, if you want to." He showed little enthusiasm at my suggestion. As I was standing there talking to him, still wounded in my pride, I sensed a voice saying within me, "Do not worry, you have done all that you can do. But come and celebrate the Eucharist for them and allow me to do what I alone can do."

A few days later I celebrated Mass there in a large lean-to hut that they used for their meetings. I remember praying, "Lord, do not allow the atmosphere inside this hut to affect me because I do not want to embarrass these poor folk in any way." I recall speaking to them on the Our Father and about the love and care the Father shows for his children. While I was speaking, I was thinking, "Why am I saying this to people who have experienced so little of the Father's love or care? Not only are they suffering from leprosy and starving, but they are liable to be bombed or killed in the course of this awful civil war."

After Mass, I came out into the sunlight and stood there with the parish catechist, who was with me. For a long time no one came out of the hut, which was strange. Eventually, after about a quarter of an hour, they began to emerge and—beginning with the children—came toward me one by one. They performed a strange little ritual uncharacteristic of Africans. They came over, took my hands, and kissed them. Finally, when all of them had done this, the leader of the village stood out in front of me with tears running down his face. Hardly able to speak, he said to me, "Father, I thank you on behalf of all of our people, that today you have brought Jesus among us once again." I, too, nearly cried.

I suddenly realized that the dark heavy cloud of depression which hung over them during my first visit to the village had lifted. The women were talking, the men were laughing, and the children were playing in the sunlight. Then I recalled the words spoken to my heart by the Lord on that first visit: "Come celebrate the Eucharist and allow me to do what I alone can do."

I have always believed deeply in the Eucharist's power to transform the lives of people, but I had never seen it so tangibly displayed as I did among those poor people that afternoon.

Those who suffer poverty can teach us many things and when we priests minister to them, the power and presence of Jesus can work miracles.

After many more experiences and examples of God at work in people's lives, my missionary career in Nigeria ended on New Year's Day 1970, when, stricken with several diseases, I was flown by medical helicopter out of the country. Eventually, the war there ended and Nigeria was reunited.

One of the joys of being a missionary is that you experience aspects of the Church which most people hardly even hear about. My admiration for the priests, brothers, and my own Vincentian confreres who worked in Nigeria at the time I was there is unbounded, surpassed only by my admiration for what the missionary sisters accomplished. People criticize the Catholic Church for its failure to allow women the freedom to work within the institution of the Church. What they fail to appreciate is that for centuries the Church witnessed the work of heroic women who set up health care and educational systems long before it was even thought of by secular powers. There were women running universities and great hospitals decades before it was even heard of in the secular world. What these women do in so many places throughout the world is a wonderful untold story.

A MINISTRY TO PRIESTS

Even before I left Africa, my missionary career was interrupted in 1968 when I was asked to do some postgraduate studies at the Catholic University of America in Washington, D.C. The contrast between village life in Africa and the academic world of North America could hardly have been greater. I arrived in July, just a week before the publication of *Humanae Vitae*. You may recall the loud public reaction the encyclical received on that particular campus. I attended the famous meeting held by theologians to protest Pope Paul VI's historic letter. Many of the big-name theologians were there and all were unanimous in their opposition to the pope and the encyclical.

I remember one of the speakers berating Pope Paul VI for daring to suggest that great abuses would follow the free availability of artificial contraception. I wonder what he would say today. Even Pope Paul could never have imagined what bitter fruits the sexual revolution, fueled by the widespread availability of contraception, would bear. If ever a man was a prophet or an encyclical prophetic, it was Paul VI and his much-reviled *Humanae Vitae*.

In early 1970, I was appointed spiritual director to the seminarians at Hallows College in Dublin. I remained at that post throughout the 1970s, a time of great change in the Church—and not all of it for the better. I was glad to be involved in the work of seminary training, even though I found the transition very difficult to make. But I could see how important this work was for the Church. My own experience of seminary life—in particular of the spiritual formation I received—is something that remains with me to this day. There is a very powerful charism in the lives of every member of a seminary faculty. It is so powerful because it is so closely connected with the person of Jesus Christ, whom the priest is to represent to the world in his ministry. I was delighted to see so many fine young men go through the program and be ordained.

During my time there we heard reports of many priests leaving the ministry. I remember asking myself what could be done about this crisis. That was the occasion of my founding Intercession for Priests, a program for the spiritual renewal of the priesthood. It was modeled on something which had been set up in the United States by Fr. George Kosicki, C.S.B. The idea of the program was to gather priests together to pray and intercede for the priesthood and, in particular, for the spiritual renewal of priests throughout the world.

Since its founding in 1976, Intercession for Priests has grown in strength year by year and is clearly meeting a need in the spiritual lives of very many Irish priests and others outside Ireland. Through my involvement with this, I began to work in a full-time ministry to priests in 1985. For some years I had worked in collaboration with Sr. Briege McKenna, O.S.C., and with the blessing of our respective superiors, we formed a team to give retreats for priests.

Since 1985, we have given retreats to clergy worldwide in more countries than I can remember. Looking back, it seems as though everything I experienced in the priesthood has been a preparation for this work and I intend to keep doing it until the Lord tells me to stop. We priests are expected to minister to everyone and to give to everyone, but there are few opportunities for us to *receive* ministry. Most clergy retreats fail to reach even a minimum standard of excellence. This is usually because of very bad customs that have grown up and been tolerated within a diocese. The retreat becomes a period of days where no one is challenged with repentance and where there is no ministry leading to a change of life. So I thank the good Lord for the grace to be involved in such a unique work.

A SUFFERING SERVANT

I feel particularly blessed to have lived out so much of my priestly ministry during the pontificate of Pope John Paul II. I remember the thrill that everyone experienced when he was elected. I was never disappointed in this great man. He was an exceptional influence on my own life and on the life of the Church, to say nothing of his historic influence on the world as a whole. I have avidly read his writings and am grateful to God for giving us a man who preaches the word "in season and out of season, and welcome or unwelcome, insists upon it." His personal holiness, physical courage, profound intellect, deep sensitivity to the needs of the poor, reaching out to the other churches, and truly priestly heart will bear fruit for generations to come. It is a great pity that much of what he has written, particularly his Theology of the Body, has been so little heeded by the Church at large.

Before seeing John Paul II at World Youth Day in Paris in 1997, a fellow priest commented to me that John Paul should retire. I forgot about the comment, which I thought was unkind, until the papal Mass in Paris, at which I was privileged to concelebrate. I was far away from the Holy Father—who was up on the stage—but I was fortunate enough to be beside a big television screen on which I could see him plainly. As he walked across the platform, bent over and obviously in pain, the priest's words came back to me and I thought, *Maybe he should retire.* But no sooner had that thought come into my mind than an inner voice said to me, "How can he resign from being a living image of my suffering servant? How can he retire from being the very presence of my crucified Son? Now is the most fruitful period of his ministry."

Old age, infirmity, and suffering are natural parts of a normal human life. We drew courage from seeing him in pain yet still proclaiming the Gospel. Such sufferings have their own power and bring their own blessing to the Church. I thank God for this great pastor and for the authority of Peter which John Paul exercised so courageously and prophetically in the world. May God continue to bless and guide the Church through the steady hand of Pope Benedict XVI!

Making Jesus present in the world, acting *in persona Christi*, is something that the Holy Spirit continues to teach me, particularly through the sacraments. I regret very much that so many priests do not seem to value the sacraments as perhaps priests once did. I have witnessed a priest deny the Eucharistic presence in a church filled with young people. During my life, I have always had great love of the Eucharist and the sacrament of Reconciliation. I have also believed in the Anointing of the Sick, witnessing many miracles through this sacrament. Any priest who lays his hands on a sick person and prays for healing can expect healings to take place. All the Lord wants from us is simple faith.

I have been a priest now for more than forty years, and I have delighted in every moment of it. I am convinced that the priestly ministry was by far the best way for me to have spent my life. If I had to do it all again, I would choose the priesthood, freely and joyfully!

෪

5

A PRIESTHOOD IN DEFENSE OF LIFE

FR. FRANK A. PAVONE, M.E.V.

I have often thought that it takes more faith to be on the priest's side of the altar, more faith to say, "This is my body" than to hear it.

The reason is that when you see a priest, you can acknowledge that through his words and actions the miracle of the Eucharist occurs. But when you *are* the priest, and you lift up the host, pausing for a moment as you look at your hands, you think: *I know these hands; I know the sins they have committed, the wrong to which they have stretched themselves out.* You then begin to pronounce the words of Christ, hearing a voice that has offended others. It takes a profound act of faith to realize that, through this sinner, God comes to his people, renewing the sacrifice that alone saves the world.

Unworthiness is an issue that everyone who even thinks of becoming a priest must deal with. Yet I have always found it helpful to put one's unworthiness to be a priest in the wider context of our unworthiness of every gift God bestows, starting with life itself. Why did he call me out of the nothingness to life? I did not ask for it or earn it. When my parents came together and conceived a child, that child did not have to be me. It could have been any of billions of possible brothers or sisters of mine. Yet, it was me. Each of us is who we are precisely because God loved and chose each of us, individually, from all eternity.

How can we be worthy of such a gift? Moreover, how can we be worthy of calling God "our Father"? The official Latin words in the Mass calling the congregation to pray the Our Father are *audemus dicere*— "we dare to say." It is, in fact, "daring" to call God our Father. We do so only because He first called us His children. We are not worthy of the gifts of faith, baptism, and eternal life. When we struggle with our unworthiness in discerning a call to the priesthood, at least it is a struggle with which we are familiar. *The fact that we are not worthy does not mean we are not called.*

FROM MATHEMATICS TO GOD

I didn't think about the priesthood until my junior year of high school. I grew up in Port Chester, New York, where my grandparents settled after emigrating from Italy. My parents, my brother, and I went to church every Sunday as a family, but we were not involved much in parish life beyond that. I attended public schools and was intensely interested in my studies. I spent so much time reading and learning on my own that I was allowed to take classes beyond my grade level, and I graduated high school a year early.

My favorite subject was math, and it played a key role in leading me to the priesthood. Math deals with the structure of the universe, of reality itself. If you follow mathematical reasoning far enough, you soon find yourself in philosophy. The concept of infinity, for example, leads you one to think about eternity. A familiarity with basic tenets such as "parallel lines never intersect" leads you to start thinking about what kind of universe it would be if they did intersect. So my studies in mathematics led me to ponder philosophy, a subject only a step away from religion.

I remember one day, at the end of an especially intense period of study, I picked up a Bible. I had never spent much time reading it, but on that particular day I experienced a sense of awe and wonder, recognizing that there must be so much knowledge and wisdom, even grace, in its pages. I picked it up slowly and reverently, and entered its sacred doors. I have never come out.

As the letter to the Hebrews states, "The word of God is living and active" (Hebrews 4:12). There is no Christian life without the word of God. I remember a talk I gave prior to entering the seminary. An evangelical Protestant friend accompanied me, and I have never forgotten the compliment he gave me. "You quoted Scripture a lot, Frank. That made it powerful. That's something you always need to do." As the years went on, I would concentrate on Sacred Scripture in my seminary studies. I came to enjoy the profound, new meaning in its pages when I was able to read it in the original languages in which it was written. (That joy is worth every ounce of effort struggling with Hebrew and Greek!) I have taught many Bible studies and Scripture courses over the years. In such courses, people often scramble to find good commentaries, only to immerse themselves in them. Although these have great value, I tried to remind my students that the most important text in the course is the Bible itself. Nothing can compare to what the Scriptures themselves say! The second admonition I give is that all theology is done on one's knees. We don't master the word of God; it masters us. And only then do we come to understand it.

CALLED BY THE MONSTRANCE

The road to the priesthood is filled with simple moments of grace, long stretches of hard work, and times of confusion and uncertainty. For me, the Eucharist and evangelization were the driving forces that led me into the seminary. It started one evening in 1975 on the feast of Corpus Christi. I was at Saturday evening Mass in my home parish, also named Corpus Christi, and after the liturgy there was benediction of the Blessed Sacrament. I saw the altar server bring out the empty monstrance and put it on the credence table. "What a privilege that boy has,"

I thought to myself. Though I was a junior in high school, I had never served Mass. Following that evening's Mass, as the host was put in the monstrance and I looked at it, I felt profoundly drawn to the monstrance and close to the Lord. There were no visions or voices, but only a profound peace, joy, and a great desire to start serving Mass. But, I wondered, was I too old? Was there an age limit? I decided I would return the next morning and ask my pastor.

Fr. Peter Rinaldi, S.D.B., was a world expert on the Holy Shroud of Turin, but more significantly, he was a saintly priest who showed everyone the meaning of holiness. When I asked him if I could start serving at Mass, he welcomed me warmly and told me I could also assist by becoming a lector. I started immediately.

Then something else started to happen. I saw a print with the image of the Lord at the Last Supper and the words, "He who eats this bread will live forever." I began reflecting more deeply on the meaning of the Eucharist. It wasn't long before I was going to Mass every morning before school and serving at the altar. The joy that came to me from the Eucharist and prayer—and the sense of personal closeness to the Lord—was so intense that I began to think, "What greater thing can I do than to help other people discover what I have discovered here?"

But this thought alone did not make me think of priesthood at first. I simply wanted to evangelize. I wanted to lead people to deeper faith. One day a woman who saw me at Mass every morning asked me if I was thinking of becoming a priest. "No," I answered, "but maybe I should think about it." The more I did, the more it made sense. When I told my pastor I wanted to go to seminary, his response was, "That is exactly what I have been praying for."

Right after high school I started my seminary training with the Salesians of Don Bosco. Corpus Christi is a Salesian parish, but I often laugh at the fact that this was not the reason I chose the Salesian seminary. Rather, I actually bought a book listing all the American colleges and universities, looked up "Catholic priesthood" in the index, and searched for the seminary closest to where I lived! It was Don Bosco College in Newton, New Jersey. When I told my pastor I was considering it, he said. "Oh, that's our seminary!"

My seminary years were full and happy, and after completing college with the Salesians, I took three years off to do other work. In the course of that work, I realized I simply wanted to be a parish priest rather than to be joined to a particular religious community. The Salesian formation I received was fantastic and continues to bless me today. But had I continued as a Salesian, I would likely have been assigned to schools or youth centers. My desire to simply to parish work led me to apply to St. Joseph's Seminary (Dunwoodie) in Yonkers, New York, the seminary for priests of the Archdiocese of New York.

In those three years before entering Dunwoodie, however, I had met a young woman with whom I developed a strong relationship. She made it clear that she wanted to get married, and for a period of time I was torn between that possibility and the call to the priesthood. I recall one moment of insight in particular that helped me resolve my painful indecision. I was in my car near the boardwalk of a resort area, and I noticed a couple walking and pushing a stroller that held their child. They looked happy. I knew that while this was a possibility for me, I also knew that it would mean that my heart would have to be focused on my wife, my child, and any other children God would give us.

It suddenly became clear. The longing of my heart was to focus on a much bigger family than I could possibly have through marriage. I wanted to reach far beyond and embrace multitudes of people whom I could love and serve, not simply as a married man might do through various forms of service, but as the primary focus of my heart, time, and energy. From that moment on, I knew I was called to celibacy, which offered another expression of love and fruitfulness.

Through all my years in the seminary, I had a map of the world on the wall of my room, and the quote of a Protestant reformer, John Wesley, underneath it, that said, "All the world is my parish." These words would help sustain my focus on the spiritual fruitfulness that could be found in the celibate life.

As every priest will tell you, seminary years go by quickly. The best wisdom about seminary was given by one of my professors when he said, "We are here not to be here but to be with God." In other words, do not get distracted either by the joys or the sorrows, the conflicts or the politics. Do the sacred work of spiritual formation and study with a tranquil focus and a keen awareness that all things pass. What liberating words they were for me to hear and reflect on.

On November 12, 1988, I had the great joy of being ordained by John Cardinal O'Connor, the Archbishop of New York at the time, and vested by my longtime friend, Fr. Benedict Groeschel. The next day, at my first Mass, my thought at the moment just before the consecration was, "Lord, am I going to survive the next few moments?" I did, of course, and began serving the people of God in the parish of St. Charles in Staten Island, New York. I very much enjoyed parish life and, among other things, learned that the best way to be a good celebrant of the sacraments is to worship along with the people. I came to see that one will be a good celebrant of the Mass to the extent that he listens to God's word with the people and worships the Eucharist he consecrates. One will be a good confessor if, while the penitent prays the act of contrition, he repents of his sins as well and rejoices in the forgiveness that he has so often received.

BUILDING UP THE FAMILY

A preeminent responsibility of the priest is to build up families. Pope John Paul II, in his 1981 apostolic exhortation on the family, *Familiaris Consortio*, calls the family a "communion of persons," and in his 1992 post-synodal exhortation on the priesthood, *Pastores Dabo Vobis*, he repeatedly uses the same word to refer to the priesthood: "communion." One of the key elements of this communion of persons is that it is a gift, a gift that flows from who God *is*—a Trinity, one God in three persons. As priests we need to have a posture of receptivity, an attitude of openness to God that says: "Lord, we're not going to build the family by our own efforts alone. Without you, we can do nothing. Give us the gift of communion." Once given, we respond by sacrificing for others. There will be no communion in the family, no unity in the priesthood, and no unity in the world unless we learn to give ourselves away.

Some young men say, "I don't think I want to be a priest." And a young woman can say this about becoming a religious sister. "I don't think I want to do that because you have to give up too much. I don't think I'll be happy giving up so much." To this perhaps the best response is, "If that's your reason for not becoming a priest or a religious sister, don't get married either, because you won't be happy in marriage." A person will not be happy in any vocation until that person learns to give him or herself away.

The reason why there is so much dissolution of marriage and the family today is because of our society's relentless pursuit of self-fulfillment. So what happens if our vocation as a married person, parent, priest, or religious stops fulfilling us in their own estimation? We often go after something else that we think will fulfill us. This is usually a recipe for perpetual restlessness. To lose oneself is to find oneself; to give of oneself is to receive. It is in this self-donation that we find fulfillment. Such self-donation is one of the geniuses of celibacy.

In celibacy, priests and consecrated religious declare to the world that, ultimately, even the vocation to marriage is directed to something more, something higher, something beyond this life. It is directed to something unseen, the gift of self to God.

A MALE PRIESTHOOD

Here we also see a key reason for the teaching of the Church that only males are called to the ordained priesthood. A first-grade girl once asked me, "Father Frank, why can't girls be priests?" How do you explain the Church's teaching on this issue to a class of six year olds? I used this example: "We're going to have a school play about Michael and Sue, who are married. On the day before the play, Michael gets sick. So now everyone is ready to come to the play and Michael can't play his part! We have to choose somebody else who can act just as well as Michael. So I looked around the class and I said: 'OK, instead of Michael let's choose Annie.' And everyone started to laugh. And I said, 'What's the matter? Can't Annie do just as good a job of acting as Michael can?' One of them raised his hand and said: 'Michael's role was to be Sue's husband. Annie can't do that because she's a girl."

So it is with the priesthood. In the priesthood, there is a marriage between the head of the Church, Jesus Christ, and the Church, His bride. Thus, the sacramental priesthood is an image of this spiritual union, a union taught in the Scriptures (see Matthew 9:15; John 3:29; Ephesians 5:32). The priesthood is a form of marriage in part because of the concept of self-donation. The more the priest gives himself to the bride of Christ, the Church, the more he reveals what it means for the family to live out its vocation as a communion of persons, freely and generously giving themselves to each other.

The priest, to be a faithful priest and fully live his vocation, is to be a *father*, not a functionary. One of the great pitfalls for a priest is when he begins to take the sacred for granted. He begins to see the Mass, or hearing confessions, or celebrating the other sacraments as mere functions more than participations in the divine. It has been a frequent prayer of mine to retain the sense of awe, of mystery, of wonder at what a priest is able to do in Christ.

I recall one occasion when we had special visitors to our parish, and one of them asked me after I had celebrated the first Mass of the day, "You don't have to stay around for the other Masses, do you?" I said yes, explaining that in the Mass the parish family is gathering. "I'm the father of this family. A priest is not only at Mass to perform certain functions; he is there as a father intensely interested in his spiritual children."

It is not any easier to raise a spiritual family than it is a physical one. Some people look at the priest and say, "Well, he's not married, he doesn't have any children, his life must be easier." This is a mistaken notion, a form of materialism, by which physical realities seen as the only real true realities. Spiritual realities, of course, are just as real, even more so! People sometimes ask, "Father, why can't priests have children?" Actually, we can—and we must. In fact, if we do not have children, born of our preaching of the Word and our administration of the sacraments, there is no growth in faith. Think of all those who hear the call of Christ or overcome obstacles to faith and prayer or receive new life by the sacraments through the ministry of priests. These are our spiritual children. If we do not believe that we are to be generative, that we are to bring spiritual children into the world, then we are practicing what might be called a "clerical contraception." We are not allowing God's creative plans to work through us. As priests, we are ordained to bring forth life and to do so generously.

THE MORAL CRISIS OF OUR DAY

After I had served happily in a parish for five years, I concluded that I was called to devote my time and energy to ending the tragedy of abortion. I had awakened to the pro-life movement in high school, and once ordained, preached frequently about abortion. The positive reaction of the people drew me more and more into pro-life activism. My pro-life work began to grow beyond the boundaries of the parish and the

Archdiocese of New York, and I came in contact with pro-life leaders nationwide. Involvement in Operation Rescue events, furthermore, inspired me to a far deeper level of sacrifice and commitment to end abortion. Moreover, seeing the pictures of aborted babies, and reading more about what abortion is, set off alarms in my conscience that made it increasingly clear to me that abortion is the overriding moral issue of our day. The children in the womb became more and more real to me, and I wanted to love and serve them and work for their protection with every ounce of my time, talent, and energy. I decided to approach Cardinal O'Connor for permission to do full-time pro-life ministry. At the same time, the Priests for Life Association, which had started in California in 1991, approached me and asked if I would be interested in serving in a leadership role.

I asked the cardinal if I could accept their offer and he gave his permission. In 1993, I became the first full-time national director of Priests for Life. It is an association of priests and deacons who make a special commitment to emphasize the Church's teachings on the dignity of human life, especially of the unborn, is recognized as the preeminent issue of justice in our day. Now, Priests for Life also accepts seminarians. In 2005, I founded a new community, the Missionaries of the Gospel of Life (M.E.V.), consisting of priests, deacons, and lay missionaries who do pro-life ministry full-time according to the charism of Priests for Life.

The priority of abortion has been articulated often by the bishops of the United States. Even so, those of us who place a special emphasis on working to end abortion are sometimes called "single issue" people. Yet, there is no other issue if there isn't life. To be sure, other social justice issues—feeding the poor, visiting the imprisoned, or assisting the stranger—are vitally important because of the dignity of the human person, but abortion is the most important because through it a person's very right to exist is denied. If we cannot defend the right that people have to *exist*, especially those who are utterly defenseless such as the preborn, then we undermine the defense of every other right. Abortion says that a human person doesn't have the right to exist. Does a poor person have the right to food and shelter? Of course. But why? Because they have a right to live. Take away the right to life, and you have taken away the basis for fighting poverty or anything that degrades the dignity of the human person.

The relationship between a mother and her child is the closest, most basic, and most fundamental relationship between any two people. So how do we allow that relationship to be destroyed without destroying every other relationship? This is where the family disintegrates; this is the very heart of the matter. If, as a society, we can't preserve the relationship between mother and child, how can we preserve the relationship between others in the family or the wider culture? How can you preserve the relationships between nations? Mother Teresa came to Washington, D.C., in February 1994 to speak at the annual National Prayer Breakfast. Addressing the president, the vice-president, and many members of Congress, Mother said simply, "If we accept even that a mother can kill her own child, how can we tell other people not to kill each other?" If the mother can kill her innocent and unwanted child, why can't that same child kill her innocent and unwanted mother, or aunt, or uncle, or neighbor, or you or me?

As a priest involved in full-time pro-life ministry, I have been told a number of times by well-meaning friends that they are glad I am happy doing "my thing," which is fighting abortion. Some of them go on to add that it is not "their thing." My response to all this is to kindly point out that whether an activity is or is not "one's thing" has nothing to do with our duty as members of the human race or the demands of justice. I fight abortion not because I am attracted to the battle, but because human life is at stake. It is a duty of conscience to defend it. I do so, furthermore, as a priest. My pro-life work flows from the very essence of my priesthood, not as something optional or extra. Most priests will not be called to full-time pro-life work, but every priest is called to a full-time, whole-hearted, active stand for life and against abortion through his priestly fathering of his flock.

DO JUSTICE!

The prophecies of Christ are heavily linked with the word "justice." Psalm 72 declares, "In his days may righteousness flourish, and peace abound, till the moon be no more," and then specifies what that justice entails: "He delivers the needy when he calls, the poor and him who has no helper . . . From oppression and violence he redeems their life; and precious is their blood in his sight" (vs. 7, 12, 14). "Righteousness" refers to an act of intervention for the defenseless. God does it for His people, and His people must do it for one another. If they do not, worship of God is pointless. This is brought out forcefully through the prophet Amos, when the Lord says, "I hate, I despise your feasts, and I take no delight in your solemn assemblies. . . Take away from me the noise of your songs; to the melody of your harps I will not listen. But let justice roll down like waters, and righteousness like an ever-flowing stream" (Amos 5:21, 23-24; see also Isaiah 1:10-17).

God's justice, ultimately, is "to destroy the works of the devil" (1 John 3:8). Those works, as Christ declared, are lies and murder (see John 8:44; Psalm 72:14 said "oppression and violence"). Nowhere is the alliance between lying and murdering more clear than in the abortion industry. Women are told their child is a "blob of tissue." They are told the abortion procedure is "safe," whereas in truth it carries untold burdens of physical and mental anguish. The pro-abortion lies are an echo of the original lie told to the first woman, "You will not die" (Genesis 3:4b). Nowhere in the world are there larger numbers of more defenseless people crying out for our intervention that at the abortion clinic. A man or woman of Christ must intervene in this modern holocaust;

a priest must "seek justice" (see Isaiah 1:17) for these spiritual children of his.

There is a story from the days of the Nazi atrocities that tells of a church along a road where the trains passed, carrying Jews to execution. When the prisoners went by the church building on Sunday mornings, they would cry out in the hope that the worshipers would hear their voices and rescue them. The noise of the wailing prompted members of the congregation to ask the pastor, "What are we to do about this disturbance to our worship?" The pastor paused and then said, "Tell the people to sing a little louder." This is the temptation today for Christians, who may think they are too busy with other things to worry about the abortion issue, too busy to worry about justice.

THE BREAD OF LIFE AND THE CHILD IN THE WOMB

A priest is a man of the Eucharist, and it is in the Mass that we touch the definitive victory of life over death: "Dying you destroyed our death, rising you restored our life." As Jesus proclaims in John's gospel, "I am the bread of life" (John 6:35). The Eucharist is the sacrifice of life and the banquet of life. Because the priest officiates at this sacrificial banquet, he is truly "Father," imparting life to all who come. The priest guards the Eucharist, which is both a human and a divine life, for it is Christ himself. The priest leads his people to adore the Eucharist and to see, beyond the appearances, the reality of life. This is why he must stand powerfully in defense of human life, which, in its initial stages, is also hidden from human sight yet no less sacred.

Just as the sacred host is "defenseless," so is the pre-born child. Just as the sacred host is sacred because it is God, so is the pre-born child the sacred image of God. If the priest is the defender of the sacred, then he is such wherever and whenever the sacred is attacked. Strangely, the same four words that were used by the Lord Jesus to save the world are also used by some to promote abortion: "This is my body." The same simple words are spoken from opposite ends of the universe, with totally contrary meanings and opposite results. "This is my body," some say, "I can do what I want, even if it means killing my child." "This is my body," Jesus says through his priests, "given up for you." He does not cling to it so that we may die. He gives it away so that we may live.

I appeal to you—a priest, seminarian, or one discerning the call—to give top priority to bringing an end to abortion because in fighting abortion we are fighting every other evil. We know that abortion leads to many other evils. But let's take it a step further. Abortion does not merely lead to other evils; it contains them in itself! Why? Because abortion holds that human life is disposable. Let us declare to our people, wherever we are, that life is not disposable. The game plan for bringing an end to abortion is given to us right in the heart of the Mass: "This is my body, given up for you, this is my blood shed for you." In other words, if we tell the mother already carrying her child that she must sacrifice herself to preserve the life of that child, and we are right in teaching her this, then we must do the same thing.

We must sacrifice our own convenience in order to save the life of the child. We must absorb the suffering because there is no way that we will root out abortion from our nations and from our world without suffering. It is the way of the cross. The false god transforms suffering into violence, whereas the true God transforms violence into suffering. We have to be like lightning rods standing up in the midst of this great storm of destruction of human life. As such, we say, "O Lord, I am willing to take some of the suffering rather than to let it be transformed into violence. I am ready to love the children who are in danger, the mothers who are in need, and a society that has gone astray. I know in loving, I will have to endure the cross. In so doing, we can transform this culture of death into the culture of life and of love.

A CALL TO CONFIDENCE

The priest must never lose confidence in the power of his ministry to transform the world. In Ezekiel, chapter 37, we read the vision of the dry bones. God placed Ezekiel before a field of dry bones, and God asked him, "Ezekiel, can these bones live?" Ezekiel answered, "I don't know." And God said to him: "Speak, prophesy, speak the word of truth to the bones." Ezekiel knew he was in a dilemma. To speak to dry bones appeared foolish, but if he did not do this, he would be disobeying God. So he spoke, and what an awesome moment it must have been. Scripture tells us he heard a rattling sound and then saw one bone begin to join to another. And God, as if cheering him on, said: "Keep speaking, speak again. Prophesy to the bones!" And the bones stood up, flesh came on them, and the spirit of life was breathed into the bones. And there was a vast army, living because of the Word of Truth.

You and I are standing in our world today over a field of dry bones, consisting of countless millions who have been killed by abortion, and countless millions of dead consciences. We do not know how or why God has placed us here, but we find ourselves in the midst of this incredible tragedy. Like Ezekiel, you and I are in a dilemma because God says to us: "Speak and proclaim the Word of Life. Keep doing it. Let nothing deter you." And we can look at God and say, "This is humanly foolish, humanly impossible. How can we transform the world from the path of death that it's on?" Others, too, will mock us and try to discourage us.

But speak. Speak like Ezekiel, for as long as you live. If you ever doubt that we can bring an end to this culture of death, this destruction of life by abortion—if you ever think for a moment that it's impossible—ask yourself: "Can a field of dry bones ever live?" Or, better yet, "Can a man who has been scourged, crowned with thorns, nailed hands and feet to a cross, pierced with a lance, has died and been buried, can such a man ever live again?"

I remember years ago praying the words, "Lord, give me more opportunities to advance your Kingdom." He answered that prayer, showed me the way in my vocation, and has given me more opportunities than I can count. He will answer that same prayer for you. Trust him without measure and follow him without hesitation. He is the God who changes doubt to certainty, confusion to clarity, and death to eternal life!

6

GOD'S GIFT TO ME

HIS EMINENCE, JOHN CARDINAL FOLEY

On Christmas day, as I knelt in front of the manger at my home parish in suburban Philadelphia, I prayed, "Lord, you have given me everything I have—my life, my wonderful family, my faith, health, and education. I want to give it all back to you." A senior at St. Joseph's Prep School, the time had come for me to make a serious vocational choice.

Little did I realize then that my decision to enter the seminary was not my gift to God but God's gift to me—and that He would at first apparently refuse my gift, as will be seen as the story of my vocation unfolds.

FAITH AND FAMILY

I was born and raised in a Catholic family, the only child of John and Regina (Vogt) Foley. My parents were outstanding Catholics in their practice and devotion, and in their desire to form themselves in the Faith. My father even took courses in the papal social encyclicals to help him as a middle manager for the Socony-Vacuum Oil Company (later Mobil Oil). My mother, who was active in parish organizations, took courses in Spanish so she could help several Spanish-speaking families who had recently moved into the parish.

My religious formation was excellent; it was never forced but was presented as a natural part of life. I was taught to say morning and evening prayers, and I witnessed the example of my parents, who knelt at their bedside every night and ended with a special prayer: "God bless Jean, Jack, and little Jackie, too, and keep them well!" (I was "little Jackie.") We said grace before meals and the Rosary on long trips in the car. Of course, we went to Mass together every Sunday and on holy days. Every bedroom had a crucifix, along with favorite religious images. We all wore Miraculous Medals, and my parents regularly went to parish Miraculous Medal novena devotions. My parents heard my catechism lessons every night and we would often discuss the implications of what I was learning.

My father had cousins who were priests. Although they did not have a direct influence on my vocational discernment, they were very interested and supportive of my vocation. I think the greatest vocational influence came from the Sisters of the Holy Child Jesus who taught me in elementary school. Mother Mary Berchmans (now Sister Elizabeth Gorvin), the school principal and my eighth-grade teacher, had a particular influence. She gave me my first copy of *The Imitation of Christ*, which I still have by my bedside. I was also richly influenced by the Jesuit scholastics who taught me in high school.

Several of the parish priests were excellent confessors and spiritual guides, and the pastor of my parish gave me some excellent spiritual books and Scripture commentaries when I was in high school and college.

At all levels of education, we were encouraged to make visits to the Blessed Sacrament, to pray the Rosary, and use aspirations as we traveled by ourselves to and from school so that we might remain in the presence of God.

A MOMENT IN TIME: EXPERIENCES AS A JESUIT NOVICE

During my senior year of high school, after Christmas dinner, I went back to our parish church and knelt in front of the manger and thanked God for all He had given me—my life, my wonderful family, my excellent education—and I said to Jesus that I wanted to give it all back to Him. I thought I was being generous, but it was God who was being generous with me.

After this moment of clear discernment, I applied for and was accepted as a novice in the Society of Jesus (the Jesuits). Though my parents knew of this decision, I kept it secret from my other relatives and my friends until I graduated from high school. Since were a close family, we all felt the anticipation of separation very keenly, but my parents supported me in any vocation to which I believed God was calling me. In fact, when I was in the seventh grade, they had given me a book by Maryknoll Father James Keller, the founder of the Christopher movement, called *You Can Change the World*. It was an appeal for people to enter professions such as politics, education, or communications—fields that could have an influence on society—so that they might be true "Christophers" (that is, "Christ bearers").

As a result of this book, I began to write radio plays on the lives of the saints because I thought that people could use the inspiring stories of good role models. When I was in high school, the guidance counselor helped me to contact officials of local broadcasting stations, and they helped me to improve my plays. They ended up being produced on a local station where I became a Sunday morning announcer at just fourteen years old. Little did I realize that I would later broadcast the activities of the pope, the Vicar of Christ, to the world.

While my parents were always supportive of my decision to become a priest, they let me know I should never feel any pressure; I was always welcome to come home. They said that the most important thing was my happiness and the fact that I would choose a path where I could do some good in the world.

At that time, Jesuit novices were not permitted any telephone contact and few face-to-face visits with family during the novitiate. So my parents and I stayed in touch by faithfully writing letters to each other. I still have all those letters, and I am moved when I read them. They tell not only news of what we were all doing, but also spiritual reflections and personal insights which remain precious to me. My time in the Jesuit novitiate lasted only six months, a period which included the wonderful month-long spiritual exercises of St. Ignatius. These were a life-changing experience. When my novice master advised me that I would probably be happier as a diocesan priest, I left the novitiate. So that I would be more certain of my vocation, I decided to complete my college education at St. Joseph's University in Philadelphia before applying for the diocesan seminary.

Thanks be to God, at that time, the university had the Sodality of Our Lady, whose rules included assistance at daily Mass, fifteen-minutes of daily meditation, daily Rosary, a visit to the Blessed Sacrament, morning prayer, and an evening examination of conscience. In addition, two hours of apostolic work were required each week, so for several years I was a volunteer teacher of religion at a school for retarded children.

One experience I had with these students contributed to my vocational discernment. The principal of the school, a religious sister, visited me and my six pupils and asked what I thought was an imprudent question: "Do you like Mr. Foley?"

One boy blurted out, "No"—and I was crushed—but then he immediately said, "We love Mr. Foley!"

The sister asked, "Why do you love Mr. Foley?"

He replied, "We love Mr. Foley because he teaches us about Jesus."

I thought, "If I wondered about entering seminary again, my doubts have been resolved."

THE SEMINARY YEARS

Later, after I graduated from college and entered St. Charles Borromeo Seminary, I thought that it took more physical effort to follow my spiritual program when I was a college student than when I was a seminarian—because I had an hour-and-a-half commute in each direction to college, while I lived at the seminary. The opportunity for apostolic work was, for me, very important—an opportunity that, unfortunately, did not exist in the seminary at that time. Both in college and in the seminary, I understood that prayer is obviously necessary to sustain apostolic activity, but I discovered that apostolic activity nourishes the life of prayer by providing further intentions and needs about which one can pray.

Though I found the atmosphere in the seminary somewhat oppressive, I was fortunate to have an excellent confessor, and he advised me to keep a list of things I thought should change in the seminary program. (I would later present this list to the seminary dean after my ordination to the priesthood.) I was also blessed to have read the book *True Devotion to the Blessed Virgin Mary* by St. Louis Marie de Montfort. On December 8, 1958, during my second year in the seminary, I privately made the act of consecration suggested by St. Louis, offering everything to Jesus through Mary—and I have never since had a doubt regarding my vocation. I have had difficult days, stressful days, and exhausting days, but never a day in which I doubted my vocation as a priest or was not deeply grateful for it.

While I am profoundly convinced of my own unworthiness to be a priest—a conviction that grows as I get older—I am even more profoundly convinced of the abundance of God's grace and of the power of the intercession of His Blessed Mother. The *Memorare* of St. Bernard remains one of my daily prayers.

Regarding celibacy, I had gone out with girls while I was in high school and college, but I could well understand why celibacy was required of priests: to imitate the example of Jesus and make oneself completely available to the service of God's people.

My role models for personal holiness were and remain my wonderful parents, persons of deep faith, and the religious sisters, scholastics, and priests who taught me or who served in the parish where our family lived. Since I had written radio plays on the lives of the saints, I was also always interested in reading the lives of the saints, which I consider the "novels" of the spiritual life, and my only current regret is that there are not more good biographies of saints being written.

Regarding doctrines with which I struggled during the time of my formation, I can say that, during the novitiate, I had tremendous temptations against faith, specifically regarding the Real Presence of Jesus in the Eucharist. I would even shake as I attempted to genuflect before the Blessed Sacrament. During that period, I prayed very hard about this issue of faith. I came to the conclusion, undoubtedly aided by grace, that just as God made it possible for human beings to transform food into their body and blood through digestion, it was possible for Jesus, the God-man, to transform food into His Body and Blood through the miracle of transubstantiation, thus making it easier for us to be nourished by His Body and Blood in the Eucharist.

In the diocesan seminary, I missed the opportunity to engage in apostolic work, and I also missed what I would call the greater intellectual freedom in college to ask questions. No questions were allowed in the seminary courses when I was a student—a practice I resolved to change if I ever had anything to do with it. I had thought that seminarians were being formed to serve an increasingly better educated group of faithful. Thus, seminarians should be encouraged to think—and be prepared for rather than potentially intimidated by the questions of others.

I found the seminary formation in obedience, however, quite helpful, and I still view the voice of legitimate superiors as the voice of God for me. Indeed, I have never been asked as a priest what I would like to do—but I have accepted my assignments without question and have always found them fulfilling and challenging. I tell seminarians today that I have never had an unhappy day as a priest—and that is true, thank God!

FROM PRIEST TO BISHOP

I was ordained a priest on May 19, 1962, by the then Archbishop (later Cardinal) John J. Krol. Cardinal Krol would later ordain me an archbishop in the same Cathedral of Sts. Peter and Paul in Philadelphia nearly twenty-two years later, on May 8, 1984. I am humbled to say that I was the only person he ordained both to the priesthood and to the episcopate. There were forty-five of us ordained to the priesthood in the same ceremony. I remember how nervous and deeply moved we were with the imposition of hands and uttering of the words of consecration for the first time with Archbishop Krol. Many of us, including myself, wept.

My First Mass of Thanksgiving was offered in Holy Spirit Church, in Sharon Hill, Pennsylvania, the parish in which I had been baptized, confirmed, and received my First Holy Communion—and where I had served Mass as an altar boy. It was truly a joy to be able to celebrate Mass with my family, my friends, and with the parishioners who had known me all my life. Just eighteen months later, I was to offer at the same altar the funeral Mass for my father who died of a heart attack at the age of fifty-seven. I was also able to return to the same church for a Mass of Thanksgiving after my ordination to the episcopate.

A very special blessing was to await me in my first assignment, as assistant pastor to Father Thomas B. Falls at Sacred Heart Church, in the Philadelphia suburb of Manoa. Father (now Msgr.) Falls had been my professor of patrology in the seminary and was "fatherly" in every sense of the word: kind, considerate, encouraging of any initiative for the good of the parish, cultured and zealous. He was spiritual director for the Legion of Mary for the State of Pennsylvania. I recall that the conversation at the rectory dinner table was always uplifting, with conversations about the apostolate, Church history, theology, or about his experiences in Rome where he had studied for almost ten years at the Roman Seminary. He later became one of four American pastor-observers at the Second Vatican Council, and was chosen to speak on behalf of pastors to the bishops of the world during the fourth session of the Council.

I have often said that an assignment to Sacred Heart parish was like going to heaven without the inconvenience of dying! There were about 1,800 families (about 6,500 people) in the parish, ninety-five percent of whom came to Mass every Sunday. During Lent, we had 2,000 people attending *daily* Mass! Our parish organizations were very active and included five praisidia of the Legion of Mary. The parish school had more than 1,000 students. I was later able to return to the parish help with Sunday ministry when I was a faculty member at St. Charles Seminary and editor of the diocesan newspaper.

When I preached at the Mass concluding the seventy-fifth anniversary of Sacred Heart Church, I clearly recalled the first year of my priesthood when the wonderful pastor and the marvelous people of the parish had furnished me with memories I shall never forget. While there I experienced an intense appreciation of the role of the priest, not only in bringing the word and sacraments of Jesus Christ but in promoting a spirit of joy and happiness in the Catholic community.

This joy and happiness have remained with me throughout my forty-five years as a priest. Perhaps my only regret is that there have not been more young men who could experience the intense satisfaction of seeing God's grace work in human lives, including, of course, our own. I wish that more young men could experience the joy of preaching, of administering the sacraments, of working with people of all ages who obviously hunger to know God better and to love Him more deeply. I truly wish that more young men would say "yes" to the invitation of Jesus and accept a vocation to the priesthood.

7

LIGHT TO THE YOUTH

FR. DANIEL ANGE

My parents, three brothers, and I had spent a peaceful evening singing canticles and praying in the little chapel of our home. We were together for the first time in a year. I had just left a boarding school in the Swiss Mountains that I had grown quite fond of, despite the fact that it seemed like an orphanage when I first arrived there at the tender age of four. I was about to be sent off to England to continue my education. On the edge of childhood, thirteen is a pivotal age and, for me, it was a time of spiritual and emotional maturity.

That particular evening, July 13, 1946, would forever be etched in my mind because of the comfort and serenity I had experienced while spending time with my family and an amazing incident that unfolded a few hours after. I was lying in bed on that warm summer evening when a clear, strong yet gentle voice summoned me from within the depths of my soul. "Daniel Ange! Do you wish to work and love and live with me? Would you?" I recall, as though it were yesterday, being smitten by an emotional upheaval. Like a true lover, God did not force himself upon me. Instead, He was most respectful of my freedom and tried to stir up a desire in me. His humility was overwhelming and just as remarkable was the fact that *He* was relying on *me*. Having been told often in primary school that I was hopeless, I had grown to believe that no one cared about me and I retreated into myself like a waif. I was a loner, given to stammering and constantly shunning company. But it was now clear to me that I, a mere thirteen-year-old, was important to my Maker. The experience completely changed my perception of God. I now saw Him as poor and frail because to love makes one poor and frail.

Until God's calling, I dreamed of becoming an orchestra conductor or a champion skier, as I was talented in both areas. Suddenly, God stepped in and showed me another path to happiness. He offered a simple suggestion, a footpath of sorts that would slowly but surely lead my way. I had lived a privileged childhood, but His voice became the North Star that guided me safely along the rugged path that was to follow. The experience completely changed my life. Never has there been any doubt in my mind that it was the voice of God Himself who I had heard.

My parents and I did some footwork, visiting extraordinary monasteries like Calcat, Solesmes, Hautecombe. Some Dominican friends invited me for a stay with them but the prospect of preaching put me off. I toyed with the idea of finding a mountain monastery that would allow me to ski, or perhaps one with a world-class organ, but I realized that I needed to devote my all to God and place my trust in Him. It was clear to me that I was called to the contemplative life. At the Benedictine abbey of Downside, in England, where I would later pursue my education, I was disappointed by the monks' involvement in teaching the young. At the time, my conception of monastic life was to be alone with God.

A few years later, at the monastery of Clairvaux on the evening of July 25, 1949, I was convinced that God was waiting for me. The community had been rebuilding the abbey with great dedication following the Nazi occupation. The abbot, Dom Jacques, was a saintly man. I wanted to follow in the Lord's footsteps under his guidance, but he thought I was too young. So my mother took me to Rome to ask for Pope Pius XII's permission to enter the monastery at the age of sixteen. "Wait quietly for the Lord's leave" was his answer. Naturally I was disappointed, but I was also deeply moved by his hands on my shoulders and the attention that he paid to a sixteen-year-old boy.

To the Monastery and on to Africa

"This is what you were born for," my mother whispered as she kissed me on the cheek and bravely turned and walked away. Night was falling quickly. A gentle, bone-chilling breeze drifted beneath my coat as I stood in front of the great dusk-shrouded cross of the abbey church. My impatience to be in the house of God and dread at leaving behind all that I held dear—music, travel, family, and above all, my parents—had torn at my emotions during the months before I was admitted to Clairvaux. I was seventeen years old. My decision had been made and I knew that I was following the will of God. With a crucifix locked tightly in my arms and my eyes glued to a statue in the garden of Our Lady of the Seven Sorrows, I wept all night. Fittingly, this was the Blessed Mother's Passion-tide Friday festival.

On the Sunday after Easter, *I* was resurrected—brought to a new life with God—when the abbot clothed me in the black robe of the Cistercian order, pending the white raiment of the Apocalypse. This day of white-clad neophytes and the open heart was later decreed Divine Mercy Sunday by Pope John Paul II. During the months that followed, I marveled at the magnificence of the liturgy and at witnessing it lived. I was wonder-struck by the splendor of truth when it is whetted by study, endorsed in adoration, celebrated in liturgy, and enjoyed for its sheer beauty.

Seven years later, I completed compulsory military service as a nurse at a hospital in Liège, Belgium. Under the influence of the famed Father Charles de Foucauld, I then founded the Fraternity of the Virgin of the Poor with other Cistercian monks in the southwest of France. Ours was a thrifty and simple monastic life. We earned our bread as laborers in the silence of the forest, home to a handful of hermits.

We were visited the following year by the first African bishop of Rwanda, who asked us to establish a mission in his country. In 1958, eight years after my first tearful separation from my parents, I cried again as my parents waved farewell from the dock in Marseilles. It seemed as though I was saying goodbye forever to my family, my friends, my country, and my culture. As my ship sailed away, I thought about the heavy hearts of the parents of so many young missionaries who had left for the ends of the earth to propagate the light of Christ. They shared in their children's sacrifice. In the 1950s, ten sailed and five landed. Of the five, three died during the first few years. Of those three, one died a martyr. Although parents and their missionary children were aware of the statistics, they courageously forged ahead with their respective callings.

Ah, Rwanda! What a thrill to discover the country of "a thousand hills and a hundred lakes." Its red-glowing or snow-capped volcanoes earned it the moniker "Little Switzerland of Africa." What joy to discover and work among the extraordinary people who would be with me for thirteen years and, in a certain way, forever. My fellow monks and I built our little community, a village of clay huts, in the side of the first sanctuary in that country to be devoted to Our Lady. This crest, known as Congo-Nile, is where the Mother of God herself appeared to schoolchildren in Kibeho. Living the rich culture and learning the beautiful language of the poor in Rwanda were among the most rewarding years of my life. I desired nothing more and would have been content to serve the rest of my life as a monk in that country, but the choice was not mine to make.

THE FIRST FRUITS OF THE CHARISMATIC RENEWAL

Twelve years after leaving for Africa, I was summoned back to Europe. I was shocked and dismayed to find that the conditions of Western youth had deteriorated rapidly in those dozen years. In complete contrast to the numbers of exuberant and hopeful African youngsters I encountered, the Western population had been declining and its young seemed shrouded in a veil of apathy.

My spirits were renewed, however, when I served on the theology faculty at the University of Freiburg, Switzerland in 1973 and 1974. I was fortunate to have the benefit of Charles Cardinal Journet's last courses. A respected theologian, Cardinal Journet is best known for his great contribution to ecclesiology, *The Church of The Word Incarnate*. At Freiburg, I also discovered the Charismatic renewal movement in its early stages. The apostolic eagerness and prayerful devotion of the youth driving the movement was contagious. I had been won over. For the first time, I actually witnessed people being physically, psychologically, and spiritually cured by the direct agency of the Lord. I rediscovered the child-like simplicity of the early prayers as described by the Desert Fathers, the monks who lived mainly in the deserts of Egypt. My baptismal fervor was reactivated by this fresh exposure to the Holy Spirit, and I had an uncontrollable urge to praise the Lord, to proclaim His truth and reveal His face, and to go forth and seek the young in order to announce His coming, or rather, His presence. After so many years of solitary existence, I was experiencing an entirely new feeling. I never would have imagined this could happen to me and I began asking questions.

During those years, I watched excitedly as the spontaneous birth of new communities and thousands of prayer groups sprouted up everywhere like spring flowers. While theirs was an oasis of life-giving joy, the appalling spiritual desert where millions of young men and women were dying of thirst could not be ignored. How, then, could the minority—members of the oasis—irrigate the entire desert? How could the vital current from the altar, where love made flesh gives life, be conveyed to the brothels where the flesh destroys love and culminates in death?

At this juncture, I was sent off to a hermitage in order to let these momentous questions rest and ripen. I spent seven long years in the solitude and silence of an Alpine valley. A relative solitude since I was with God, the angels, the saints, and the entire world. A relative silence since I could hear, echoing in God's heart, all the young people of the world crying for help. It was the Eucharistic experience of the burning bush—God hearing the call of His people, Moses seeing God looking upon their distress, and then the Lord sending Moses back from the desert to the Chosen People in Egypt.

In my solitude, I felt increasingly torn between divine plenitude in the very body of God and the knowledge that an entire generation was hurtling away from the Church. I was drinking from the fount and multitudes were dying of thirst. My apostolic vocation was born of my monastic life. It was no accident. I loved to climb up the mountain at night, after receiving Communion. I could see the lights of Monaco glittering on the horizon and I could not help but think of the distress of the young people who had fallen prey to drugs, prostitution, and all of the caricatures of love.

So, I started my new life, my new ministry, by accepting invitations from the Charismatic renewal. The aim of my participation was to connect the novelty of the movement to age-old Catholic tradition. I was expected to provide the countless new converts with a basic knowledge of the great theology of the holy Church. Being at the crossroads of the old and new, I had the opportunity to graft all of those young shoots onto the trunk. That meant leaving my hermitage to go on tour with renewal groups like the *Beatitudes* and *Le Pain de Vie* (the Bread of Life). Having done so afforded me the advantage of getting to know the groups' founders well, too.

Eager young people who had found their way back to the Church attended our gatherings. My gaze, however, was riveted on the empty seats. Time and again, I would ask myself, "Where are all the others? So many children are missing the roll call! How can I reach the more remote ones?" Much like the signal Paul received from the young Greek (Acts 16:9), I finally received my signal one day. I thought, "I, too, must pass through Macedonia." My signal came in the form of a letter from a pupil at a technical college. He wrote, "Come to my school! Three thousand, five hundred pupils! No one to listen to us, no one to comfort us! Oh, Church! Why do you forsake your children?" My first direct call from Western "pagan" youth broke my heart. I told my bishop and my prior about the letter and both said that ignoring such an appeal from the Lord was out of the question.

Scared and shaking, I set out for the technical school in question. It was 1981. Before I knew it, I was marching through all the classes at the school. Set loose in another world with no direction, I was terrified. Contrary to those I had met in the new charismatic communities, these fourteen to eighteen-year olds were far from won over. They eyed me cynically. The adults had warned me, "Not a word about God. Stick to social and, possibly, sexual problems." Sex was no longer taboo; it was now God who was taboo. After the visit to this first school, I was fielding calls from more and more schools. How could I remain silent? A godless desert was tearing me away from my desert with God.

Ski slopes beckoned through the windows of a secondary school in Mégève, France one Friday afternoon, but the students were glued to their chairs, spellbound by tales of God told by fourteen-year-old René Luc. The teachers were astounded. We needed a thousand René Lucs. This would later become my apostolate, Jeunesse Lumière, which means "youth light." Now an international Catholic school of prayer and evangelization, its simple premise remains as valid as ever—to form young people and send them to spread the word of God to other young people.

MY PRIESTLY PENTECOST

To help me prepare for this new apostolic ministry, my prior suggested that the time had come for me to be ordained a priest. A monk is limited to the devotion and discipline prescribed by his order, but as an ordained minister, I would be able to carry out the teachings of the Church. How could I listen to a young person confide his entire life story and then leave him there as if on the pavement, without giving him what his heart had always most profoundly waited for—the loving kiss of God, that is, His sweet pardon? How could I continue to proclaim Jesus without offering His Eucharistic presence? I suspect it would frustrate the young person and the Savior to not experience a mutual and sacramental encounter. I became desirous of the priesthood because I knew that it would abet my mission with the young.

My bishop proposed ordination by the Holy Father at the international Eucharistic congress in Lourdes, but that blessing was not to be. Pope John Paul II was still recovering from an assassination attempt when I was ordained, July 23, 1981. In a message to the newly ordained priests, however, the pope offered his blessings. So, in my priesthood, I am the child of not only the Blood of the Savior but also of his servant John Paul. Before 100,000 delegates representing every diocese in the world, I—who had imagined a small, quiet ceremony—was ordained by the Holy Father's delegate, Bernadin Cardinal Gantin of Bénin. An African bishop had received my monastic vows in 1958 and another would transmit me into Jesus' own priesthood. Cardinal Gantin and I would be profoundly linked forever. He invited me to celebrate morning Mass with him each time I passed through Rome. He also added my name to the list of all those he had ordained and he vowed to me that each day he would say those names. For my part, I love saying in the full Eucharistic prayer, his name, as is done in the Byzantine rite.

As a priest, nothing impacts me more than giving the sacrament of God's pardon. If sin ages, forgiveness rejuvenates. Reconciliation is God's sacrament of eternal youth. In the sacrament of Reconciliation, I am a surgeon of the divine aesthetic. I restore the souls and therefore the faces, disfigured or simply lined by sin, to their beauty as children of God. Nothing could be as momentous, therefore, as hearing the final confessions of the two people on this earth who meant the most to me, my parents.

Even though his knees were sclerotic, my father had set himself to dancing in the garden singing with full voice "Jerusalem, Jerusalem, leave your cover of sadness and dream of the beauty of the glory of God." He had worked a great deal in Jerusalem on the reconstruction of the Basilica of Eleona. The work—and the Ascension and return to glory of Jesus—caused his excitement for the other Jerusalem. His Lord no longer delayed in calling him there.

Ten days before my mother died, she swore to me, "When I meet Jesus again, I want there to be no sadness in his eyes, only joy! Therefore, on the off chance, I want to give him now all of my sins!" I obliged. My mother's desire was an obedient response to God's word that death can come at any time (1 Thessalonians 5, 2-4). I was on a mission in Libreville, Gabon, Africa when, like a thief in the night, the Lord took my beloved mother. I'll always feel the loss of her deeply, but I take great comfort in knowing that the Lord was smiling when she united with Him for eternity.

A SCHOOL OF HOLINESS

In 1983, two years after my ordination, I launched my school of prayer and evangelization. Jeunesse Lumière would be the first Catholic school of evangelization in Europe. A number of subsequent proposals were the catalyst to spreading the apostolate to many locations around the world. Priests from each school meet annually to share our experiences and focus on specific features like internationalism, the contemplative dimension, the fraternal dimension, and the apostolic dimension. We learn from each other and also from our students. Our schools are places of continual birth. God forms me through these young people and I receive each student as a treasure of love, a gift from His heart, a living word and symbol of the face of Jesus. As a priest, proclaiming the Lord is much more than announcing the "good news." It is a *Presence* to offer, an *Encounter* to foster, and a *Person* to cherish.

Preaching the Gospel is like placing in God's arms one of His children who did not know Him. Evangelizing is giving spring water to those dying of thirst. It is changing their hearts—poor, cracked, dried-up wells—into inexhaustible fonts of running water that lay, not beside, but within them (see John 4:4-42). Evangelization means opening the future to people for whom death is only death and who rush madly at it or who stumble round as though blind. Much more than just revealing what lies ahead, it also means giving them the means to succeed, the keys to the Kingdom of God.

Preaching the Gospel is a wonderfully liberating task. Chains are broken, moorings are cast away, prison doors are smashed down, and locks are unlocked in order to let captives see the light, breathe the bracing air and enjoy the open sea. Through the Gospel, Satan's victims are snatched from his clutches and set free from his toils and from the slavery of drugs and ideologies. (I have in mind the image of those brave American soldiers entering Auschwitz and Dachau.)

FROM NATION TO NATION AND GENERATION TO GENERATION

Ministering abroad and sharing from parish to parish the greatness and beauty that I have witnessed is one of my deepest joys. My international, or inter-ecclesiastical, pilgrimages are designed to adore the presence of God and honor His mother, while dispensing the great tradition of Israel and the Church to the next generation, which has been totally uprooted and severed from its vital loam. Revealing Bernard, Francis, Dominic, Teresa, Catherine of Siena, John Bosco, and so many friends of God to young people is tantamount to assisting in the recovery of their squandered legacy. Quoting as contemporaries John Chrysostom,

Augustine, and John of the Cross is like giving back to younger generations what has been stolen from them. It is part and parcel of our future if we are to meet these saints in heaven. Today's youth, however, must be made aware of what God has given us through his servant John Paul II and of what He will continue to give us through Pope Benedict XVI. It is pure gold in the form of a genuine deposit of fabulous spiritual and doctrinal riches that have not been disclosed to our younger generations. This requires reinstating in God's children the legacy of which they have been stripped.

As if the vast meadow of Lourdes had become the launching pad for my international missions, my ordination in front of delegates from around the world was the starting point for my global ministry. Immediately after I was ordained, I was sent to Canada, Poland, Lebanon, Ivory Coast, Cameroon, and more than forty other countries for a total of 240 missionary visits, each ranging from three days to three weeks. Travel has provided me with an extraordinary insight into the Church. I have been privileged to see her in so many facets, from meetings with parents to teachers and catechists, from children to the elderly, and from the handicapped to the imprisoned. I have also been blessed by encounters with almost all the bishops of the dioceses through which I have passed. In addition, I've been on retreats with priests and seminarians. Most of my invitations come from new communities and spiritual congregations, and most of my meetings are with young people. Because of this, I am very optimistic about the future, which is not on the distant horizon but very much within our grasp.

No longer do I simply believe in the great springtime announced by Pope Paul II, for I actually see it. I can fully endorse his words, "I see the dawning of a new spring morning heralding a glorious day." At the 1991 World Youth Day in Czestochowa, John Paul II exclaimed, "Mankind is on the threshold of a new spiritual age." Afterward, I addressed 200,000 young Polish members of the charismatic renewal who had been standing for hours on end in the pouring rain. Just as a tree must first take root in the desert in order to spread its boughs without running the risk of being uprooted by the first storm, I could not have had such a wonderful ecclesiastical experience had I not spent thirty years in the solitude and monotony of a humble monastic life rooting in the Gospel.

In order to be fully present at my first ministry, Jeunesse Lumière, and to preserve precious moments of meditation in the hermitage, which is near the school, I restrict my evangelizing trips to no more than eight days per month. Alternating meditation and teaching with apostolic missions is both trying and soothing, but the two complement each other well. Whenever I leave my brothers in the hermitage, I suffer from the Jonah syndrome. I would give anything to remain quietly with the Lord and my brothers, yet my heart longs to share what it has gathered. Likewise, I feel shattered when I must return from a mission venue, even after responding to the needs of young people in distress. However, my heart must return to the solitude that I had been missing throughout the mission. Through an accumulation of trials, the heart grows in dedication and willingness to submit.

How rewarding it has been to have met, throughout my twenty-five years of holy ministry, four or five generations of youth! When I can take part three years running in a gathering of young people and deliver several lectures each time, it amounts to teaching the equivalent of the curriculum absorbed in the course of a basic retreat at Jeunesse Lumière. Admittedly, I still get stage fright. I have never quite gotten used to addressing large crowds, and I panic at the possibility of offending or disappointing. So, before each lecture I whisper, "Lord, do not look at my sins but behold the faith, the yearning and the needs of your flock! Do not disappoint their expectations!" I am always touched when young people invite me to their religious profession or their first Mass, or when they introduce me to their spouse or spouse-to-be. Likewise, I am moved when young couples return to thank me for urging them to remain chaste until their wedding day because they have realized God's blessings for their patience.

EVANGELIZATION THROUGH BOOKS AND EMAIL

Another avenue of evangelization I have begun to pursue is the written word. Writing is a long-term form of evangelization because, for one thing, books take a long time to write. From insemination to flowering, the process requires the patience of a farmer. It often takes years to write a book. Also, written words are indelible. Lectures, sermons, and talks pass fleetingly, but printed material is more durable. Providence has afforded me the time to write nearly fifty published works which, it is my great hope, will lead many closer to the Lord and his Church. The advantage of evangelizing through writing is that I can work on my own. All of my major books date back to my years of isolation. Even today I write during periods of hermitage or retreat.

How moving it is to think that pages I write on a mountain pasture will one day find their way to a multitude of readers in different countries. I receive so many letters from readers that correspondence (especially email) also becomes a means of listening to and speaking with young people. Genuine dialogue takes place over months and sometimes years. The thousands of little secrets confided in me nourish my prayers. I deposit these intimate—and sometimes painful—notes in the chapel's tabernacle, or under the corporal if I am celebrating the Mass alone, for a period of "Eucharistic incubation" before answering them. I call it my "pneumatic microwave oven" (from the Greek, *pneuma*, spirit).

One of my great passions is the bodily unity of the Church. The complete union of our sister Churches, Orthodox and Catholic, is much closer at hand than some "technical hitches" might lead us to believe. Our common struggle for, quite simply, the vitality of the Faith commands that we unite our efforts. Furthermore, Christ's prayer for unity, being that of God Himself, cannot possibly fail to come true, even if our infidelities sometimes delay its realization. I feel compelled to preach the word to defenseless young people in Eastern countries as well. They gape spellbound at the West, which is seduced by liberal materialism. Because their natural immune system has been neutralized by communism, they fall easy prey to pornography and drugs. Like all of us, they need the same courage as the martyrs of whom they are the offspring, children of their tears, their blood, their prayers, and their love.

THE STRUGGLE TO PROTECT LIFE AND REDEEM LOVE

As Pope John Paul II repeated over and over, the age of martyrs has begun again. Although underhanded and less brutal, both the East and West have entered a new era of Christian persecution. Eastern martyrs show us the way in this apocalyptic struggle between the angel of death and the Prince of life, between lies versus truth, hatred versus love. I feel personally very much involved in this struggle. Most of my public lectures are focused on the mystery of life, with close reference to all the people, especially the young, who fight so bravely from dawn to dusk to protect life wherever it is most frail and vulnerable—and thereby most threatened.

Pope John Paul II's encyclical letter *Evangelium Vitae* is the rousing charter of our struggle. It unites us as one behind its author, the undisputed champion of life, who is acknowledged as such well beyond the boundaries of Catholicism and even Christendom. What joy it is to belong to such a Church, the only one to bare its fangs like a lioness protecting her cubs when it comes down to saving man from his fellow man.

Inseparable from life is love. When love is squandered, life itself is laid waste. When love loses its value, life loses its flavor. Sullying love means stifling life. On all fronts, I have tried to protect our youth from the criminal pornography mongers who make as much money out of sex in the United States as does the arms trade. My fight has led to my being viciously slandered by the proponents of unbridled sexual freedom on a French national television station at a peak viewing hour. (While I was acquitted by justice, no acknowledgement was ever broadcast.) The aim of most of my teachings for the young and of my four books on the subject is to shed God's light on the endangered natural wonder called sex.

In this ruthless struggle, we must be ready to give up our lives to save life and to shed our blood in order to protect love. Let all those who suffered martyrdom at the hands of Nazism, Communism, and Muslim fundamentalism—not to mention those in Lebanon and Rwanda, many of whom I have known personally—be our guides. During the Rwanda genocide, my spiritual father, Msgr. Louis Gasoré, was killed while baptizing a child and blessing his murderer's family. Like a good shepherd, Paul Késenne, a Belgian abbé and friend, was slain because he refused to abandon his flock. In my parish, thousands of faithful were savagely slaughtered while worshiping the Holy Sacrament. These martyrs did not die in vain. I pray that their sacrifices guide and encourage us as we spread the truth.

Father, we ask for the courage to lay down our lives, that we might preserve life. Make us worthy of being heralds of Your glory. Give us the strength to endure the new wave of persecution aimed at the Sacred Heart of Jesus, and help us discern and answer Your call to Holy Orders.

8

GOD MADE ME AN OFFER
I COULD NOT REFUSE

FR. ALBERTO R. CUTIE

After my father was sent to prison for the second time, my parents knew the family had to move.

When the communist dictatorship took over Cuba in 1959, the atheistic state closed Catholic institutions and expelled hundreds of priests and religious. On two separate occasions, my father was unjustly imprisoned, and it was clear my family could no longer remain there.

My entire upbringing was deeply impacted by that move. This "exile experience" affected not only my family but also millions of other Cubans who, to this day, are dispersed all over the world. If my parents had stayed in Cuba, they would have been unable to practice their faith freely. We children would have been unable to attend a Catholic school or receive religious education. The entire family would have been denied a host of basic freedoms, including choosing a profession or owning a business.

In 1967, my parents and eldest sister were able to leave Cuba and go to Spain. They arrived with only one Cuban penny in my father's right pocket. Other Cuban families already in exile there helped them find a place to stay. My family lived in Madrid for almost two years, until they reunited with my grandparents and extended family in Puerto Rico, a United States territory. I was born there in 1969, an American citizen.

Many Cubans came to call Puerto Rico home because of its proximity to Cuba in language, culture, and climate. Most, however, eventually made their way to Miami, where the greatest concentration of Cuban exiles in the world have established "a home away from home." My family arrived there when I was seven.

I am a Cuban-American, a "hyphenated" American. I am an American citizen by birth, but my culture, background, and roots are Cuban. My great-grandfather fought in the war of Cuban independence at the end of the nineteenth century. This heritage, this identity, has been reinforced in every way by my vocation to the priesthood. The Cuban church and its unique history are a part of who I am. I am a priest in the United States of America, and I feel very much part of the Church in this country, but my heart is always connected to the experience of the persecuted Church that lives in Cuba.

It is important to point out that this experience is certainly not unique to me. I am only one of approximately forty million Hispanics that live in the United States and have brought the experience of traditional, family-oriented Catholicism with them. That influence, I believe, is why the Church in the United States is becoming more traditional, devotional, and, hopefully, more Catholic.

I was raised in a typical Catholic (Cuban!) home. I do not recall *ever* missing one Sunday Mass as a child and I was blessed to have a mother and father who practiced what they preached. My parents did not "shove church down our throats," but the obligation of striving to live a good Catholic life was always present in our home.

My father was a professional and very dedicated to his work as a mechanical engineer, yet very simple in his ways. My mother was always a devoted mother and wife who put morality and the practice of religion as top priorities in our home. The older I get, the more I am convinced that my vocation stems from the good example of my parents. When I think of role models in my vocation, my mother and father always come to mind first.

Before one can accept the gift of a vocation to the priesthood, one must accept the vocation to live an authentic Christian life, as my parents did.

My two sisters—one older and one younger—went to Catholic schools, but I went to public school after the second grade. Even so, I never stopped receiving religious instruction in my parish and at home.

I remember my preparation for First Holy Communion. The religious sister took me aside and asked me to recite my prayers (the Our Father and Hail Mary, among others), but I had just barely begun speaking English. I will never forget that American Franciscan's smile as she gently said, "You can say them in Spanish. I think God understands." I was very relieved, to say the least.

I know there are more than a few horror stories about first confession, but mine was one of the most positive spiritual experiences of my childhood. That year was the first time my parish offered the sacrament face-to-face, and so we were given the option of kneeling behind a screen or going around it and seeing the priest—and having him see us! My plan was to stay hidden, but as I entered the confessional—which I had assumed would be dark and scary—I saw a very bright light shining through a stained glass window behind the priest. Apparently, I had walked too far into the confessional, right past that screen.

I still remember his smiling face as he invited me to sit in front of him. I cannot recall what sins I confessed at age seven, but I know I experienced something I had never felt before. I was sure I had received the grace of God through sacramental absolution. If I were to pinpoint an experience in my childhood that led me to appreciate the priestly ministry, it would have to be that day—my first time in the confessional.

It was not until much later, when I was in high school, that I began to consider the priesthood. I had been actively involved in my parish youth group for some time and began assisting on weekend spiritual retreats. These experiences of a lively faith and youthful Church helped me to see the priesthood as a truly attractive vocation and way of life. The many young priests I had contact with at that time, who remain good mentors and friends to this day, helped me to understand the priesthood as a life of joyful service.

I must admit that was not my earlier impression. When I was in grade school, it seemed to me that priests were somewhat removed and tended to be, to put it frankly, a bit boring. I always admired their work and recognized they represented God, but I considered them as other-than-human. I never perceived the priesthood as an exciting and challenging life. It was not until I actually began to meet priests and interact with them that the priesthood really began to mean something more to me. I started to realize the priesthood was so much more than what I had seen as a child, and I immediately became attracted to ministry and priestly service. I came to understand that priests accompanied people at the most important stages of life: the beginning, the end, and everywhere in between. Being a shepherd means to be with the sheep in good times and bad … that made priesthood all the more interesting to me.

That is not to say the decisions and choices were easy to figure out. I knew there was something supernatural pulling me in that direction, but I never felt pushed by any human being to consider the priesthood.

In many ways, I was an unlikely candidate. I was not an altar boy. I had not attended Catholic schools. No one in my immediate and nearest extended family had ever been ordained or professed vows as a religious. (I did have one great-great uncle who was a priest and eventually became an archbishop.) I am convinced my call to priesthood was totally God's idea, not mine. If it had been up to me, I am sure I would have devised some very different plans.

FROM DISC JOCKEY TO SEMINARIAN

At the time I told my parents I was thinking about becoming a priest, I was a sophomore in high school and working on the weekends as a disc jockey. That meant spending a lot of time playing music at parties. I think it may have shocked them more than a little, when their teenage son came in one day and "dropped the bomb" that he was considering entering the seminary.

My parents responded with faith. Whatever their concerns may have been, they gave me their support. I remember telling my mother first and her sending me to my father. They both agreed, "If it is what God wants, and you are going to be happy, that is what we want for you." As the news of my decision spread, many of my friends were amazed and even shocked, but most of them knew of my relationship with the Church and my interest and involvement in my faith. Some were not surprised at all.

My friends did wonder about one thing: the promise of celibacy. The "not having sex" thing. I will never forget when an astonished friend asked, "You're going to give up girls?" I answered, "We're all going to give up girls when we get married. For you, there will be one girl; for me, it will be the Church." I am not sure I convinced them, but my high school friends were supportive of my vocation to priesthood.

Another incident stands out from this time. It was Lent and I was going to confession in my home parish, St. Timothy, in Kendall, a large suburb of Miami. I remember there were many people waiting and I was just looking for the shortest line. I walked into the confessional and was greeted by a priest I had seen before. At the end of my confession, I told him I was thinking about the priesthood and asked him to pray for me. He assured me of his prayers and asked me my name. When I said I was Alberto Cutie, his eyes opened wide and he proceeded to ask me where my parents were from. As it turned out, this priest had been my father's confessor and high school chaplain in Cuba. He knew my whole family. He was also the spiritual director at our local college seminary.

Shortly after that confession, I began spiritual direction and a process of discernment with the help of this holy priest. Early in this process he told me, "Albert, the girls will always be there, and the attraction will not go away, but God is calling you to serve Him." These words helped me greatly in understanding what a vocation to priesthood entails. It was not about giving up your manhood or disconnecting from reality. Priesthood was presented to me as a real challenge and choice, a desire to serve God above all things. Lifetime decisions are not easy to make, but I have never forgotten my process of discernment and the many graces I received. It was truly a blessed time. It took years of youth retreats and mingling with young and old priests and religious to discover that God wanted me to follow Him in this unique way. But when I discovered my vocation, I felt a great sense of peace and satisfaction that served as a supernatural confirmation of my call. I was certain this is what God wanted from me.

I always describe my vocation as God's invitation. *God made me an offer I could not refuse.* At some point (I don't remember a specific time, date, or place), God called me to share in His Son's priesthood, to be His servant and to belong exclusively to Him and to His people. Why? It's a mystery. I still joke around with friends and say to them, "If I was God, I would not have chosen me to be a priest, but since I am not God, I guess I had to obey His wishes."

Over the years, I have come to realize that the "why?" or "how?" is not what ultimately matters. What really matters is that God offered me an invitation that was so irresistible, that I could not help but respond. God called me to be part of a unique and special marriage: the union between Christ and his Church. He called me to be an instrument of His grace and love for His people, to refresh and heal a tired and broken world, to speak on His behalf and, most of all, to be another Christ (*alter Christus*).

By inviting me to His holy priesthood, the Lord has called me to be a man of faith in a world full of doubt, to build bridges where walls have been erected, to bring those weighed down by the death of sin to the joyous life of grace. He has called me to be a "man for others" in a world full of selfish men; to belong completely to Him and to His people, without reservation; to unite my heart with those who are in greatest need; and to try lifting them up when they are down. The Lord has also called me to be a "sign of contradiction," to live the Gospel in a radical way, to be a co-worker of His kingdom, to share His freeing truth with my brothers and sisters. In the words of Blessed Teresa of Calcutta, He calls me to be faithful, even while not always successful.

Still, the greatest part of God's tremendous offer to me, in calling me to His priesthood, is the fact that, as unworthy, limited, and sinful as I am, he calls me to say the Lord's words at the consecration: the words which make Him present sacramentally in our world. Each day at the altar, I have the privilege of saying: "Take this, all of you . . . This is my body . . . This is my blood." Then, too, one cannot forget the words through which he imparts his healing forgiveness to souls: "I absolve you of your sins." The gift is in the fact that, for a moment, his words are my words and my words are his.

What a gift, what an offer! There is no way I could refuse that!

THE "JOHN PAUL II BOYS"

I always thank God for my seminary years. Looking back, I have to say they were the most challenging and formative of my life. I attended St. John Vianney College Seminary in Miami (about ten minutes from home) and St. Vincent De Paul Regional Seminary in Boynton Beach (about an hour away). Both were pretty much filled to capacity with an excellent group of candidates for the priesthood, and both were blessed with an equally good formation team made up of excellent priests, and religious and lay professors.

As I reflect on my seminary years, I often associate them with the pontificate of Pope John Paul II and his extraordinary impact on the Church in the contemporary world. During the years following the Second Vatican Council, many seminaries and religious orders went through a profound period of turmoil and confusion. When I entered the seminary in 1987, there were still a few professors who embraced the failed theories of the immediate post-conciliar years. They had a very hard time convincing my generation, though—the "John Paul II boys."

As young men in today's turbulent and often confused world, most of us wanted structure and discipline. We desired a Church with tradition and clear expressions of faith. We wanted Latin in the liturgy and Gregorian chant. We were a bit tired of guitar Masses and somewhat banal liturgies. I believe most of our professors and those entrusted with our formation did not fully understand this. They often accused us of being "ultra-conservative" and were often defensive if we supported Church teaching or expressed our dissatisfaction with their vision of the Church. While I cannot remember anybody in my seminary experience who was markedly liberal or heterodox, there was certainly some confusion among our superiors as to what they wanted us to absorb during those vital formation years.

It struck me as strange that when the pope released an encyclical, there was silence about it in the seminary. If there was some psychological survey or study from a secular university, however, we were fed the results as manna from heaven. In a sense, the students who were part of my seminary years had to dedicate themselves to "auto-formation." If we wanted to know what the Church really taught, we had to look it up and study it ourselves. In my own experience, I believe this was the Holy Spirit's way of making me more involved in the process of my formation. As a result, I became hungrier for the truth and the richness of the

Church's Magisterium and Tradition. I discovered the Fathers of the Church and the great spiritual masters throughout the centuries. Some of my classmates would ridicule me by saying I was a "walking encyclopedia of the Church's documents." I am not sure this was the case, but I certainly spent those years trying to read everything the Church had to say about everything.

I had no time to become bitter about the limitations of the seminary. When I began theology, my fifth year in the seminary, my father was diagnosed with terminal cancer, and this made those years a sort of internal Calvary. I was a dedicated student, but I also had to be a dedicated son. My younger sister was only a teenager and my mother needed her son's support. All through my father's illness, even when he was unable to work, my father always encouraged me to stay in the seminary and continue my priestly formation in spite of the financial hardships this caused our family. I also remember receiving much support from priests, my pastor, and the staff at our seminaries.

I was ordained on May 13, 1995, at St. Mary's Cathedral in Miami. It was a beautiful day, not only because of the great solemnity and reverence with which our ordinations were celebrated, but also because it was the feast of Our Lady of Fatima. I have always had a great devotion to the Blessed Mother, and I felt privileged to be ordained on one of her feasts.

When Archbishop John Clement Favalora greeted us and our families before starting the entrance procession, I remember he said to our parents, "We will take good care of your sons." My father had a bird's-eye view from heaven, since he had died two years before, but I very much felt his presence on that glorious day. My mother, grandmother, sisters, and family were in the first row. I was reminded of the fourth and eighth Stations of the Cross: an group of devout women crying as I was about to lay down my life!

As the litany of the saints was chanted, we lay prostrate on the floor. It was a time of recollection and deep reflection. My whole life flashed before me. I understood the great mystery I had been called to share in—to "lay down one's life" (John 1:15). I think about that ceremony often, but especially each year at the Chrism Mass when we renew our priestly promises. My first Mass was the following day, Mother's Day. It was wonderful, filled with solemnity and shared with countless brother priests, religious, and laity who had accompanied me with their love and prayers throughout my seminary years. It was like coming home after a long time away. It felt as though I had always celebrated Mass. Funny, I thought I would be nervous, but I felt right at home. God meant for me to be there ... a great sense of peace.

As a deacon, I had served at St. Mary Star of the Sea Parish in Key West, the southernmost parish in the United States and the closest to Cuba, only ninety miles away! After being ordained a priest, I was sent to the northern end of the archdiocese: St. Clement's in Fort Lauderdale.

St. Clement's was filled with challenges and adventures. The people of the parish were extremely loving and welcoming, and my fellow priests were first-class. One of the most memorable experiences my first week as a priest was walking through the church parking lot one morning and hearing a lady calling out, "Father! Father!" I just kept going. I was not used to being addressed as "Father," especially since I was only twenty-six, and most of my parishioners were older than I was.

I was so happy to finally be a parish priest. I taught in the parochial school, assisted in every aspect of parish life, and spent a lot of time working with the youth program—trying to inspire young people to stick to their Catholic faith.

Priesthood, like all of life, is constantly evolving and developing. As the years go by, I understand that my concept of priesthood has also grown. While priestly ministry is as diverse as the men ordained to live it, we all have a common mission and vocation. Through my work in both secular and Catholic media, I have been privileged to share the gift of priestly fraternity with priests throughout the world. I have discovered that we all share the same struggles and frustrations, without forgetting the many joys and satisfactions. The brotherhood of the Catholic clergy is a sacramental bond—an unparalleled unity of mind and heart. I confirm this more and more each day. Only a priest can truly understand another priest. That is why it is tragic when a priest does not value or exercise priestly fraternity.

OUR GREATEST TREASURE IS OUR FAITH

I am often interviewed by reporters who are curious about some aspect of my work in the media. They often wonder, "The Church teaches this, but what do you think personally?" I always respond the same way: I think what the Church thinks. It is a simple concept but a difficult one for many to grasp. *Sentire cum ecclesia* ("to think with the Church") is not just a result of some sort of training; it is the gift of faith, which manifests itself in the life of someone who opens himself or herself to the mystery of God. If you love and understand the Church's teaching, you begin to think with the Church, feel with the Church, and understand reality with the eyes of the Church. It is very sad to find men of God—even at the highest levels—who do not think with the Church or feel with the Church. The Catholic faith is a treasure entrusted to its care by our divine Lord. We must all safeguard it and proclaim it as it has been revealed to us.

Our greatest treasure is our Faith, but people today often do not have time to discover it. That is why I consider the *Catechism of the Catholic Church* to be one of the most effective instruments of evangelization for today's world. The more the faith of the Church is known, in all of its splendor and with real clarity, the better for all of humanity. People today need clarity; they seek guidance. If the Church does not present the truth about God and man to today's society, nobody will. This, to me, is one of the driving forces of my priesthood and, in hindsight, likely a strong reason I felt called to the priesthood. I love to teach the

Faith. I see the sanity and peace that comes to those who believe in the revealed truths and who strive to live them. As a priest, few things bring me greater joy than seeing a lay person make the logical connections between the faith and the living of their every day life.

Pope John Paul II set a great example of the courage it takes to have a "dialogue with the world" in order to communicate truths of the Faith. No one did this more effectively than that great communicator of our times, a man I believe will be named a Doctor of the Church. John Paul's encyclicals and apostolic exhortations are a wealth of knowledge and faith to the entire Church and world. My favorite is an apostolic exhortation titled *Salvifici Doloris (On the Christian Meaning of Human Suffering)*. This document reveals much about John Paul's commitment and love for those who suffer: the poor, the sick, and the downtrodden. It shows his great compassion and is a reflection of what suffering has meant in his own life. On a very practical level, this document on suffering has helped me personally and in my priestly ministry. I believe that if people can find value in suffering—which is surely to come everyone's way—they possess a secret that can help them weather any storm. In fact, I believe the Church's teaching on the salvific value of suffering is one of the best kept secrets in the Church today. If this message alone could be preached with greater frequency, I believe we would have more vocations, more Catholic couples who are faithful to Church teaching in the area of sexuality and the indissolubility of marriage, fewer people leaving the Church for other faiths that offer a softer, and perhaps "exciting" faith experience, and so much more.

On several occasions, I had the privilege of being in the presence of Pope John Paul II: in my first year in the seminary during his 1987 visit to Miami, at the pallium ceremony on the feast of Sts. Peter and Paul in the Vatican in 1996, and in a private audience while taping a documentary on the Vatican for Catholic television in 2004.

In his later years of illness and physical limitation (in contrast to the robust health he enjoyed in his younger days), John Paul remained a great teacher for humanity. Ever the witness of the gospel of life, he stressed that life is sacred and valuable—even as so many want to do away with it. This ties in to what I consider one of his most outstanding contributions: his great humanity and closeness to the people of God.

I think that St. Pius X (the saintly "Pope of the Eucharist") and Blessed John XXIII (*il Papa bono*) have much in common with John Paul II. These three holy men have made a lasting impression on me because of their simplicity of life and great spiritual caliber. I also find them to be very practical men who did not allow their office to get in the way of their very unique, yet strong, personalities. Pope Benedict XVI was always someone i admired. From my first days in seminary, I knew that the pope had a German theologian in the curia, named Joseph Cardinal Ratzinger, who was a quiet, yet firm, servant of the truth. My seminary buddies and I devoured the *Ratzinger Report* since it was published and we enjoyed every one of its pages. It was a natural reaction to the more progressive forces that some of our seminary professors represented. We wanted tradition, Latin and solid theology—Joseph Ratzinger represented all of that. In Pope Benedict, our often confused world has a clear vision of who Christ really is; not the distorted versions which are so prevalent today.

LIGHTS, CAMERA . . . EVANGELIZATION

My first love is being a parish priest. The celebration of the sacraments and the direct contact with people are sources of great blessing for me. However, my job description changed very suddenly in 1998 when the international Spanish-language television network Telemundo, owned by General Electric and NBC, asked me to become a talk-show host. They wanted a priest to host a talk show with the traditional and spiritual elements popular among Hispanics. As a direct consequence of my involvement in television, and with the approval of my archbishop, I eventually began to also work in radio and the press.

I had always admired the late Archbishop Fulton J. Sheen—perhaps the most prominent "media" priest in Catholic history. He was often called "the Microphone of God." His autobiography, *Treasure in Clay*, was the first book I read when I entered the seminary. I never imagined that I would be one of his successors in the secular television world. Between Archbishop Sheen's last television broadcast and the introduction of *Cambia Tu Vida con el Padre Alberto* ("Change Your Life with Father Albert"), the show I was asked to host, there was not a single priest hosting a major program on a national secular network. I began to think about this as more than just an invitation and to see it as an act of God. We are all familiar with what the secular media does to present its own version of the Church, and especially the priesthood. Now I was being given an opportunity to portray the true Church—with all her teachings—in a very unique environment: a talk show. Imagine entering millions of homes each day, without even knocking on the door!

After spending quite a bit of time in prayer before the Blessed Sacrament, I consulted with my spiritual director and with a very holy bishop. Both encouraged me to accept the job. I will never forget the urgency in the bishop's words: "Albert, you *must* do it." When I asked my archbishop for permission, among the interesting things he told me was, "If Jesus were here today, He would probably have hosted a talk show to get the message to people." I found that humorous, but eventually confirmed the value and wisdom behind those words.

During the first two years of production, I taped 220 shows each year while continuing my regular parish work as parochial vicar at St. Patrick's in Miami Beach. The show then became a weekly live program, and my bishop named me general director of our Catholic radio stations in the Archdiocese of Miami, which broadcast in English, Spanish, Haitian Creole, and Portuguese. I also began to write a daily advice column, a kind of "Dear Abby" with a spiritual twist. All this interaction in the media has also put me in contact with the entertainment industry—both celebrities and executives. I view this aspect of my ministry as one of the most important reasons for my presence in media; it is my small contribution to the evangelization of the general culture.

In spite of all my activity in the media, I still enjoy more than anything else the celebration of the Eucharist and the sacrament of reconciliation. It is through the sacramental life that God's people are sustained and healed of their sins. Our sacramental life is what makes us uniquely Catholic.

THE PRIESTHOOD AND THE CHURCH

In every institution, there are levels of commitment and differences among members. The great challenge I see in today's Church is a deep apathy and a lack of vision at every level, from the hierarchy to the people in the pews. The timidity of many bishops in confronting the challenges to the Faith and the undermining of the sanctity of marriage demonstrate that the foundations of the Christian life need to be radically strengthened. The greatest scandal in our Church is not the behavior of a few immoral priests; it is our lack of fidelity to the Gospel of Christ and our unwillingness to seek holiness with all our strength and resources.

Christ's promise to St. Peter when he established the holy Catholic Church ("and the gates of the netherworld shall not prevail against it"; see Matthew 16:18) gives us the certainty that the Lord will always guide his flock and never abandon his people. Nevertheless, ours is a crisis of human shepherds. We need spiritual guides who are willing to serve the people of God in today's tumultuous world.

The priest shortage is not our biggest problem—the quality of priests is much more important than the number. The abuse scandals in the beginning years of the new millennium can actually produce blessings for the Church, if we pay attention to the Holy Spirit's voice amidst all the pain. I hope the scandals do not teach us only about lawsuits and settlements but rather push us to do everything possible to have a more devout clergy, men committed to living and proclaiming the Gospel of Christ.

We must rid ourselves of the pessimism pertaining to celibacy. Priestly celibacy is not what keeps young men from entering the priesthood; however, unhealthy environments where there both a lack of clarity as to what is expected and lack of proper integration of the sexual gift keeps good candidates away from our seminaries or makes them return home. When priestly celibacy is lived authentically as a sign of the kingdom, nobody seems to question it. It is with scandals and immoral behavior that celibacy loses its validity in our society.

A SIMPLE, YET PROFOUND, SPIRITUALITY

As a diocesan priest, I always tell people I have three loves: the Eucharist, our Blessed Mother, and the Church. This is a simple, yet profound, spirituality. These are the three loves of all Catholics, but they have a very special place in the heart of a priest.

If we have a love for our Lord present in the Eucharist (in his body, blood, soul and divinity), our participation in the holy sacrifice of the Mass and our times of Eucharistic adoration will be the center of our faith. Our love for his Eucharistic presence is essential to living in union with Christ. Saying the Mass each day has always been a priority for me, no matter where I may find myself in the world. To this day, I have never taped a television or radio program without first saying Mass. A priest must have a Eucharistic heart.

Devotion to our Blessed Mother is not an option for today's Christian. Loving Mary is part of loving our divine Lord. In order to be a disciple of Christ, one must follow Mary's example, since she was the first disciple. Mary is also "Mother of Priests," and she stands with us, just as she stood with her Son at the foot of the Cross. I have celebrated the Mass of the Blessed Virgin Mary every Saturday since the day I became a priest. Just as Sundays are the Lord's Day, so is Saturday the day of our Blessed Mother.

Without a deep and authentic love for the Church and its teaching, the priestly ministry dries up and becomes sterile. Our love for the Church should come through in all we say and do. Knowing its teaching, and making it part of our lives and the lives of those we minister to, is certainly a priority in the life of all priests. Our love for the Church allows us to suffer for it and with it.

Being a Catholic priest in the twenty-first century is a great adventure. While the challenges may be many, I feel blessed and privileged to be a priest of Jesus Christ today. I feel a sense of overwhelming gratitude to God for giving me the gift of a vocation. I know that nothing in this world could have fulfilled me more or could have been as exciting!

ঌ

9

A Vocation from Birth

Archbishop Elden Curtiss

I am one of those rare priests who knew from a very early age that I was born with a vocation to the priesthood. I do not make this statement out of pride or any credit to myself, but simply as a matter of fact. I have not heard many seminarians or other priests speak about such an early call to priesthood, so I conclude that it must be rare. From my earliest conscious moments I knew that, somehow, I was going to be a priest. In fact, I cannot recall a time when I did not want to be a priest. My mother told me that I practiced celebrating Mass when I was just four or five years old. She knew I was eventually going to be a priest because of all the signals I gave early on, and always encouraged me to pursue this goal.

As a young child, I was always very much at home in church. Sometimes when other children were fidgeting in the pews and distracted, I would be still, intrigued by what was going on at the altar. Outside of church I played as aggressively as other children, but in church I knew that something special was happening. And I was always very comfortable around our parish priests and was at ease with them as I was growing up. I had an affinity with them that was rather unique for someone my age, and especially for boys who tended to be somewhat shy and reticent around priests.

Now, after nearly fifty years in priestly ministry, I realize that it was an extraordinary and unmerited grace to have avoided the struggle that comes with the discernment of a vocation to priesthood. This is especially true in this media-saturated and sexually-permissive time in which we live. I am convinced that, proportionate to Catholic population, there are as many vocations today to priesthood as there has been in past centuries. I think the recent drop in vocations in our own country is due to various cultural conditions that are drowning out the "still small voice" that calls men to this glorious vocation in the Church.

A VOCATION NURTURED IN THE CRADLE OF THE FAMILY

My father was born in Baker City, Oregon, where his grandfather had migrated from Illinois in the Gold Rush days. My mother was born in Slovenia, but her family migrated to this country when she was three years old. Her family settled in Rock Springs, Wyoming, where my grandfather worked in the local coal mine. When my grandparents were able to save enough money, they moved to Eastern Oregon to a little community on a mountainside that reminded them of Slovenia. My father and mother met in Baker City where she had come for nurses' training. They were married in 1931. Both of my parents came from a long tradition of Catholicism and were active in their parishes. My mother, in particular, was a very prayerful woman who taught her sons how to pray and to be close to the Church. My three brothers are practicing Catholics to this day and are very much involved in the life of their parishes.

When I graduated from grade school, a priest friend suggested that I should enter the seminary high school. My mother, however, said no to this proposal. She thought it was better for me to stay at home during my high school years to attend the Catholic high school in Baker City, so that I could have the influence of the family in my life. It was not that my mother did not support my vocation to priesthood—as did my father, though in a less verbal way. They both continued to encourage me to think about the becoming a priest. My

mother had an uncle who was a priest and an aunt who was a
religious sister in Slovenia. My grandmother, who lived near us,
was even more delighted at the possibility of having a priestly
vocation in the family. Their conviction about the importance
of priesthood came from a deep faith in the Eucharist and a
profound understanding of the special calling of a young man to
participate in the priestly ministry of Jesus Christ himself.

Now as I look back, I think my mother's decision to have me
attend the local Catholic high school rather than a high school
seminary was a good one. During my high school years, family
and friends were important for my formation as a person. They
helped me address the myriad of challenges that came my way
during these formative years. However, once I had graduated
from high school in 1950 my mother was very supportive of me
going to the college seminary, if that is what I wanted. My father,
even though he remained quiet about these matters during these
years, told me afterwards that he was very pleased that I had
decided to go to the seminary. I received nothing but constant
support from my parents, my three younger brothers, and my
extended family. This support was able to contribute to my
already enthusiastic embracing of seminary life that followed
over the next eight years.

I have been asked by various people at different times
whether there was any period of doubt in my mind during the
seminary years. The short answer is no. I knew I belonged in
the seminary from the first moment I arrived there. Even in high
school, when I was dating a girl that I was fond of, my thoughts
about priesthood were always present. I explained to her one
time that even though we continued to date I was definitely
planning on going to the seminary. I also recall a conversation I
had with my spiritual director, a Sulpician priest, early on at the
seminary about the question of priestly vocation versus marriage.
He told me that this was a decision that I would have to face,
and one that I would have to make before I was ordained. My

decision had already been made, despite knowing that marriage
was a beautiful vocation.

LIFE AT ST. EDWARD'S SEMINARY

When I entered St. Edward's Seminary in Seattle as
a college freshman in 1950, I had an immediate sense of
belonging despite the fact that the seminary life was very strict
in those days. I simply liked seminary life: I enjoyed the classes,
especially the study of the philosophy of St. Thomas Aquinas.
It was the first time I had been exposed to his teachings in any
substantial way and the clarity of his thought was exciting. I
began to see how a good foundation in philosophy formed the
basis for solid theology. Because of my love of philosophy I did
well in my studies.

Also I liked very much the seminary routine and structure.
My days were made up of prayer, the celebration of the Eucharist,
studies and recreation. I am able to say that these disciplines,
learned early, have served me well all my life. In the years of
priesthood that followed—as a parish priest, a seminary rector,
and a bishop—the daily routine I learned in the seminary served
as the foundation for my daily routine throughout my life. With
the other seminarians in St. Edward's, we learned how to "get
things done" by following a regular schedule. This is the reason,
despite challenges that have been mine these past thirty-one
years as a bishop, I have been able to continue my duties with
much enthusiasm and energy that comes from a balanced life I
learned at the seminary. I cannot underestimate how important
these disciplines, learned during those eight years formative
years in seminary, have been to my life and ministry as a priest
and bishop.

The seminary also grounded me in the identity that would
be mine with Jesus through the sacrament of Holy Orders.
Even though our theology in the 1950s was pre-Vatican II and
very traditional regarding the person of Christ and the nature

of the ministerial priesthood, I have come to appreciate the perduring value of the theological truths that I learned in my seminary years.

The mystical dimension of the priesthood, which was downplayed to some extent after Vatican Council II, is in fact essential to understanding ministerial priesthood and one's role as a priest. The writings of Pope John Paul II, specifically the document *Pastores Dabo Vobis ("I Will Give You Shepherds")*, have been especially important in refocusing our attention on the sacred dimensions of priesthood. Pope Benedict XVI continues to help us recover the patristic roots of the theology of the sacrament of Orders. The mystical relationship between the priest and Jesus has again emerged as the central dimension of priesthood.

During our seminary days in the 1950s we pursued an intimacy with the Lord in the Eucharist which led us to an intimacy with his people. We strove to learn how Jesus responded to people in all kinds of circumstances, and we meditated on the awesome reality that God so loved the world that He sent His Son as a man to minister to us. We priests have the unique privilege of continuing this priestly ministry in our own day to our own people. This mystical dimension of the priesthood was and continues to be essential to understanding the ordained priesthood and what it means to be a priest of Jesus Christ.

Following the Second Vatican Council, there were some who emphasized the role of priest as one who leads the congregation in the Eucharist as a family meal rather than as the paschal mystery of the suffering and death of Jesus, which is essential to the Eucharistic celebration. Pope Benedict XVI is striving to bring us back to this essential understanding of the Eucharist. I personally think that the Church and vocations to priesthood will be energized by this re-orientation by our Holy Father to the essential nature of Eucharist and priesthood. Young people today seem to recognize this need to identify the ministerial priesthood with the ongoing ministry of Jesus with his people. This is a healthy development in the life of the Church, and for vocation ministry everywhere in the world.

THE CHALLENGES THAT FACED US AFTER VATICAN II

Since I was ordained to the priesthood in 1958, four years before the beginning of the Second Vatican Council, I was very much a part of the pre-Vatican II Church. I did make the effort to read and try to understand the documents of the Council that were promulgated. Early on, I began to be concerned about the interpretations of these documents offered by some, and about certain proposals to the Church that were being made "in the spirit of Vatican II." With some effort, I embraced the reforms in the liturgy which the Council encouraged. I also experienced some enthusiasm about the possibilities of involving lay people in more profound ways in the mission of the Church. At the same time, I was becoming increasingly uneasy with the theologians, catechists, and liturgists who were calling not only for a *renewal* of the Church but for a *reformation* of the Church, including her liturgy and many of her teachings.

This was the reason that in 1970, when I was pastor of a rural parish in eastern Oregon, I responded to call from the monks of Mount Angel Abbey in St. Benedict, Oregon, to be an instructor at their seminary. Bishop Francis Leipzig, of Baker City, allowed me to be assigned to Mount Angel seminary as director of field education, as a consultant to the seminary program, and as a high school seminary religion teacher. The seminary at that time included a college preparatory high school, a college seminary program, and a graduate school of theology.

Abbot Damian Jentges, O.S.B., told me he was concerned about the loss of support for the seminary by bishops in the area, and especially about the consternation of Archbishop Robert Dwyer of Portland regarding the seminary program. At that time, seminary formation was based on the *Ratio Fundamentalis*, a decree from the Congregation for Catholic Education, following the Second Vatican Council that guided seminary formation. This decree outlined general principles but left it up to individual countries to develop specific guidelines for their seminaries. Most seminaries had jettisoned the old seminary system even though they did not have a new system in place that had been tried and tested. As a result, seminary education was very much in flux. I proposed to the administration that the seminary should be a microcosm of a diocese with clear lines of authority and structure, as well as promoting clear fidelity to the magisterial teaching of the Church. I proposed that the faculty be concerned not only with the documents of the Second Vatican Council, but with those of all the previous general councils of the Church. This position was not accepted by all the administrators and faculty in the heady atmosphere following the Council. However, on January 1, 1972, at the age of thirty-nine, I was appointed president and rector of all three divisions of the seminary.

It was a difficult task to reconcile the views of the reformers on the seminary faculty with those of the traditionalists, trying to encourage both sides to read and accept the conciliar documents as written, and the post-conciliar documents that were gradually published. At the same time I had to resist the tendency of certain faculty and staff members to use selective quotes from the Vatican II to develop inappropriate speculations about the "future church" that they were promoting. It was important for the traditionalists to accept all the documents of the Council, and to accept the fact that major reforms in liturgy and parish structures and the role of the laity were here to stay. At the same time it was important for the reformers to accept the fact that it was the same Church as before, but with new emphases and developments. My goal was to maintain a creative tension between opposing views about interpreting the Council, without compromising the traditions of the Church and her magisterial teaching, and at the same time not compromising the legitimate reforms of Vatican II.

MY CALL TO BE BISHOP

When I was appointment Bishop of Helena in 1976, at the age of forty-three, the previous seminary experience helped me cope with the tensions that were present in western Montana and throughout the church in the United States. I had been hesitant to accept the call to be bishop because of my age and the responsibilities that I would have. I delayed my response to the papal representative for several days. I finally decided that it was the Holy Spirit who was calling me to the episcopal office through Pope Paul VI, and that it was the Spirit who would guide me as a bishop.

I would spend the next seventeen years as Bishop of Helena. During this time I was supported very much by the post-conciliar documents that flowed from the Second Vatican Council which helped us to interpret authentically the original documents of the Council. There were people in the Diocese of Helena who had a vision of the future church that was democratic, ecumenical, and free of clerical domination. There were those who wanted to question Catholic tradition, especially certain doctrinal and moral teachings; there were those who emphasized the church of the laity, sometimes at the expense of the ordained priesthood; and there were people who were unhappy with any efforts they thought were contrary to their interpretation of the reforms of Vatican II.

On the other hand, I encountered many faithful people throughout the diocese who had been battered by speculative agendas which were not in sync with magisterial teaching. They had endured a number of priests who took certain liberties with the liturgy. They had suffered from a growing feminist movement that abhorred paternalism and male authority in the Church. Traditional, conservative people were struggling to preserve the unity of their Catholic faith and their connection with the larger Church. And there were tensions caused by a kind of fundamentalism which relied on private interpretation of the Scriptures and the gifts of the Spirit, as well as a growing kind of congregationalism that opposed any authority but that of the congregation. But in the midst of these various extremes were the majority of priests and people committed to the Church who wanted to live as authentic Catholics in a changing world. These were the people who helped me hold the church of Western Montana together despite the different ecclesiologies, expectations regarding ministry in the Church, and ideas regarding future directions that the Church should take.

Over the years I have been asked what it is like to be a bishop, to be one of the successors of the apostles. From a purely human point of view, there is (or should be) some trepidation about the call to such an office. The responsibilities of leadership in the Church that are his, and the call to faithful service for a lifetime, are challenges that any churchmen should not take lightly. This was part of the reason for my initial hesitancy when I was asked to be a bishop. But what I have discovered over these years is that, when we learn to do the will of the Father as did Jesus, the life and ministry to which we are called not only is possible but actually becomes a joy. I have always enjoyed the people to whom I have been called to serve, even when there have been disagreements and tensions. I think my own sense of humor and love for the Church combined with a sense of respect for people, have helped me weather many storms over the years. And despite the disappointments and failures I have experienced, I have been able to maintain a sense of gratitude for the call that Jesus gave me so many years ago, to follow in his footsteps as a priest and then as a bishop.

I have always been convinced, and I have shared this conviction with many people over the years, that if we pray every day, and exercise regularly, we can take anything in stride. Also,

I am convinced that our own minds are not the final arbiters of truth. To be faithful Catholics means that we accept the Church as a gift of Christ to us. We accept the wisdom of the Church, even when we cannot always understand it or appreciate it. We should stay with the Church no matter what happens. I have learned that when I am faithful to the magisterium of the Church, and support Sacred Tradition, then I am at peace with myself and the people around me. To be an authentic churchman means to be in union with the Church in all matters of faith and morals, and to love the Church as the bride of Christ.

SUPPORTING VOCATION MINISTRY IN THE CHURCH

A few years after my priestly ordination, I was assigned as Catholic chaplain at Eastern Oregon State University. I came to see that many young people were in fact hungry for truth and meaning in their lives, despite the many distractions that they faced. They were searching for a spiritual foundation and for holiness. I realized that many young men and women would be open to vocations to the priesthood and consecrated if they were invited and supported in that call, and if they had role models that they admired. I contend that the current vocational crisis in our country is due partly to the fact that we are not encouraging young people to consider a priestly or religious vocation. We Catholics have to ask young people who we think would make good candidates whether they have ever thought about priesthood or consecrated life. People have to be asked and they have to be encouraged to pursue the vision.

As I mentioned before, I believe that as many men today, proportionately, are being called to priesthood as in past generations. In addition to the fact that the call is being drowned out by the noise and distractions of our culture, we members of the Church are not nurturing vocations as we did in the past. During my years as a seminary rector and later as bishop of

Helena, it became apparent to me that the older "feeder" system for identifying and fostering vocations—namely, the priests and religious sisters and brothers in our schools—needed to be replaced by lay people who took their places as teachers. When I was growing up, there was no way that I could have escaped the sisters and priests in our classroom who invited me to think about priesthood. It was a common practice back then to be asked by clergy and religious to consider the priestly vocation. But now we need a new "feeder" system that includes Catholic parents, school teachers, and parishioners who are willing to pray for and solicit vocations. If we want vocations to priesthood, then all our laity, as well as our priests and religious, need to ask people to respond to the call. We also need to teach our young people to pray and be devoted to the Holy Eucharist so that the call to them will not be lost. A closeness to the Lord in the Blessed Sacrament will, among other things, inspire our young men to consider a call to priesthood. We cannot have Eucharist without priests.

During the time I was bishop in Helena, I was elected by the United States Catholic Conference of Bishops (USCCB) to chair their Vocation Committee. This position gave me the opportunity to address vocations issues on a national level and encourage my fellow bishops to make stronger efforts to develop vocation ministries in their dioceses. Later, as Archbishop of Omaha, I served six years as episcopal advisor for Serra International, an organization of lay people whose primary purpose is to support vocations to priesthood and consecrated life. It was my privilege, in many places throughout the world, to emphasize the fact that the Eucharist, which is the very life of the Church, is available to us only through ordained priests. Fostering new vocations to the priesthood is not an option for the Church, it is a necessity. And this task, although primarily that of the bishop, is one that has to be shared by the priests and laity in our dioceses. Young people have to be personally asked to consider a vocation to priesthood and consecrated life. They have to be encouraged to try out life in the seminary or novitiate. They have to be supported and helped along their journey to priesthood and religious life. What I have learned these years is that there will be a lack of enthusiasm for vocational ministry, and it will flounder, unless: 1) a significant number of priests in a diocese are committed to the priesthood as the Church defines it and are happy with it and are willing to promote it; 2) women religious support the ordained priest as the Church defines it; and 3) lay people support vocations to priesthood and consecrated life as the Church defines them.

A VISION FOR THE FUTURE

I often think of the words of St. John's gospel, "For God so loved the world that he sent His only begotten son" (John 3:16). The Father was willing to send his son, Jesus, into a messy world because He loved the world. A priest or bishop has to learn to live with this messiness and yet has to be able to call people to holiness in the midst of it. I am becoming increasingly more impressed in recent years with all the young people who are responding to the call of the Lord to serve Him and His people. The power of the Gospel is being revealed, conversion is taking place all around us, and the fruits of the Spirit are manifest in the lives of many people. This is the reason that, despite being tired in body in these latter years, my spirit is constantly uplifted when I minister the sacrament of Confirmation to young people and when I ordain new priests. The presence and power of the Holy Spirit in my own life and ministry, and the gifts of the Spirit in the lives of the people around me, give me much hope for the future.

In 2008, I will celebrate thirty-two years as a bishop and fifty years as a priest. The thoughts that I had as a young boy about the priesthood have been confirmed and enriched a thousand times over. I now believe, more than ever before, that a close relationship with Jesus in the Eucharist; a strong devotion to

Our Lady, given to us by Jesus as our own Mother; and a total fidelity to the magisterial of the Church are keys to a fruitful and happy priesthood. Despite all the challenges I have faced, my life has been one of great happiness. I would not trade my experiences as a priest for anything else in the world. The Lord has supported me and helped me deal with every crisis in my life and ministry. The gifts of the Holy Spirit, shared so generously with me, have helped me see beneath the surface of things to the deeper realities of life. I have learned that my own human gifts, helpful as they have been in my ministry, have not been nearly as important as the gifts of the Spirit. Because of my own weaknesses and sinfulness, I could have never survived these many years in ministry by myself. I have been able to walk with the Lord and to be aware of His providential care and love in my life. For this I can only say, "All glory be to the Father, and the Son, and the Holy Spirit, now and forever. Amen."

ॐ

Editors' Note: Archbishop Curtiss served as episcopal advisor to Serra International for six years. He continues to be involved with this worldwide organization of Catholic men and women who are committed to promoting vocations to the priesthood and consecrated life—and to growing in their own holiness in the process. For more information on Serra International, visit www.SerraInternational.org.

10

A CALL TO COURAGE

FATHER JOHN HARVEY, O.S.F.S.

In 1980, I responded to a call that would change my life and the lives of so many others in a profound way. Nearly four decades before, I had already answered the Lord's call to the priesthood. This new call came from Terence Cardinal Cooke, then the Archbishop of New York. At that time, the cardinal noted that Catholic men and women with same-sex attraction had no shepherd in the Church to meet their needs, to minister to them and call them to holiness. As His Eminence was aware of the work I had done in this area, he contacted me and the organization Courage was born. I would experience God's grace in ways that I never imagined when I was first ordained thirty-six years earlier.

My story is one of influences and inspirations, all guided by God's powerful hand. Its interest lies in the work that our good Lord ultimately called me to do. The Holy Spirit calls each of us to some unique and meaningful work. We find the greatest peace in this life when we say yes to that call. Each day I pray, "Yes, Lord, yes," and "Thanks, Lord, thanks!" This is the story of my yes, for which I give God great thanks.

My story begins with adversity that led to blessing. I was born in Philadelphia in 1918, the third of four children, and my mother passed away when I was only four. In the second grade, Sister St. Magdalene would read us stories of the saints, and by doing so she nurtured the seeds of a priestly vocation. She told us how St. Ignatius Loyola persuaded St. Francis Xavier to enter the fledgling Society of Jesus, how St. Francis gave up a chance to be a professor at the University of Paris to become a missionary in Japan and India, and how he died at the age of forty-six. I wanted to be like him, a missionary priest! All through grade school, that thought never left me.

I came to view the nuns at my school, the Sisters of St. Joseph, as taking the place of my mother. They taught me, knew me, and, I believe, loved me. Even when trying to teach me to write with my right hand—I was naturally left-handed—they did so with patience and gentleness. On one occasion in eighth grade, a dear old nun was disciplining several of us for making noise and it was my turn to put out my hand to be smacked. I held out my right hand, trying to protect my left hand (after all, I was a southpaw pitcher!). She said softly, "Please put out your left hand," and then added, "Some day you will be using your right hand for better purposes." "How does she know I want to be a priest?", I remember thinking. I was happy that she knew.

After the eighth grade I took the scholarship examination for the local Jesuit high school, but I did not think my father could afford to send me there. This was during the Depression, and he had three other children to support. The school awarded five full scholarships, but I placed sixth in the ratings. I was not crushed, however. I had decided I wanted to go to Northeast Catholic, which was run by the Oblates of St. Francis de Sales. An older friend told me the Oblates were good teachers. At the time, I knew nothing about St. Francis de Sales. It turned out to be a good choice, one that would direct the course of my life.

During high school, my confessor was a diocesan priest that most of my peers chose to avoid because of his standard penance—a full Rosary! This did not dissuade me from seeing him each week, and I benefited from his good counsel. For example, when a young Oblate student-teacher unfairly gave me a punishment of conjugating French verbs, my fellow students suggested I refuse to do it. I took the matter to my confessor, and while he agreed I had been treated unjustly, he told me to remember that Jesus was treated unjustly to the point of death on the Cross. He said to accept the punishment for love of Christ. A lesson in obedience was instilled in my young mind, a lesson which would serve me well throughout my life.

I was attracted by the gentle spirit of my Oblate priest-teachers. I turned down an offer of a full scholarship at St. Joseph's College, a Jesuit institution. The Oblates of St. Francis had a hold on my heart. Fr. J. Francis Tucker, the first American Oblate, spoke each year at our student retreat, and I was deeply impressed.

A few days after graduation, I was called to the high school to be interviewed by an Oblate. "You must know our life is very challenging," he said. I answered, "Yes, I know," thinking about the missionary activities of St. Francis Xavier (who was actually a Jesuit).

When I applied to the Oblates I was given a thorough physical exam. The doctor said I had a heart valve problem and was underweight. He told me that I might live to be eighty or I could die young. I wondered whether the order would accept me. Feeling discouraged, I walked over to the high school and ran into the principal, Fr. William Stahl, O.S.F.S. He assured me, "We have many bad hearts in our house. Go to the novitiate." In whatever condition, my heart was at home in the Oblates of St. Francis de Sales. I have never regretted my choice.

ST. FRANCIS DE SALES SHAPES MY LIFE

I entered the Oblates novitiate in Childs, Maryland, on July 6, 1936. Despite the negative medical report, I had no health problems—even though the novitiate was much like boot camp in those days. The very first morning, the dormitory bell made sure we were in chapel by six o'clock for the Angelus. Following the Angelus, everyone was silent for some time, and I couldn't understand why Mass didn't begin. I soon came to learn that the daily schedule included spiritual reading, meditation, Mass, and prayer.

During that first year we read and meditated on Holy Scripture and the writings of St. Francis de Sales, particularly his *Introduction to the Devout Life*. In the past six decades, I have gone over this volume countless times. I came to use it along with the Twelve Steps at Courage meetings. It took years for its lessons to shape my inner life. I found great strength in St. Francis' discussion of the virtues of humility and gentleness, as well as in his words on anxiety and discouragement. Even recently, these lessons helped me in very personal circumstances, such as when I was the victim of a pickpocket in Rome and when a pastor denied me the privilege of delivering a eulogy at a close associate's funeral. Perhaps the most important virtue I learned from St. Francis de Sales was obedience to the desires of my superiors. During my novice year I was taught one does not wait until a superior *demands* obedience before carrying out his request.

After my novitiate year, I headed for the Catholic University of America in Washington, D.C. During my two years of philosophy studies there I had an outstanding teacher, Dr. Rudolph Allers, who taught psychology in such a way that I decided to seek a master's degree in it. In one semester Dr. Allers focused on the freedom of the will, using St. Augustine's *Confessions* as the center of his discourse. This psychiatrist, with a wonderful background in philosophy and theology, made me think about ways of integrating the insights of psychology with those of philosophy and theology.

The next step in my academic career was to enter a program for a licentiate degree in theology. My interest in psychology remained high, however, and in the summers of 1942 through 1944, I completed the psychology courses I had begun during my academic years but could not finish due to my theological coursework. I was on track for the priesthood, and I was ordained on June 3, 1944. Having reached the priesthood, I looked forward to integrating the perspectives I had learned in psychology with pastoral theology.

In the fall of 1945, I took my final required course for a master's degree in psychology. The professor, Gregory Zilbourg, was a distinguished Russian scholar who opened up my mind still further. I remember also the foreword of a book on child psychiatry in which the writer said that too often in the healing professions (medicine, psychology, and psychiatry), one speaks in terms of success or failure when really a better way of looking at difficult situations is to see things as open to improvement. The word used was *amelioration*, i.e., to make things better, even if only gradually. This concept would inform my later work in difficult pastoral situations.

At this point I began teaching remedial reading back at Northeast Catholic High School in Philadelphia, the school where I was introduced to the Oblates of St. Francis de Sales as a teenager. I had a desire to work toward a doctorate in psychology at the University of Pennsylvania. In 1947, however, the superior of our house of formation in Washington, D.C. informed me that the Oblate Council wanted me to go back to Washington to study for a doctorate in moral theology. The Provincial Council had plans to begin a school of theology for Oblate candidates for priesthood, and they needed faculty to staff it. I was surprised by the request, which was not a mandate. I really wanted to study psychology while teaching high school in my hometown. I shared my dilemma with an elderly Irish nun who replied, "Father, consider that your provincial, his councilors, and your Washington superior all want you to study for a doctorate in moral theology so that you will be able to teach in your own seminary, and you hesitate? Don't you see that their desire is for you God's explicit will?" I knew she was right, and the lesson of obedience again came to the fore. I accepted my superior's request.

One year later, in 1948, I received a telegram from the provincial requesting that, as I worked on my doctorate, I would also teach two hours a week at Dunbarton College of the Holy Cross in Washington, D.C. I really didn't want to do it, but—again, following St. Francis de Sales' advice concerning a superior's "request"—I agreed with the hope it would only be for one year. I ended up teaching moral theology there until the college closed in 1973.

THEOLOGY, PSYCHOLOGY, AND ST. AUGUSTINE

At the beginning of my second year in the theology program, I had to select a doctoral thesis in moral theology. I proposed to the academic dean Fr. Joannes Quasten the topic of healing grace. He took my outline but said that I did not have the necessary background for the topic and suggested he assign me one. Two weeks later, I began working on *The Moral Theology of the Confessions of Saint Augustine*. Father Quasten told me to do it in any form I desired, adding, however, that any quotes from the *Confessions* had to be substantiated by the Latin footnote at the bottom of the page. In writing about the moral content of this book, I came to understand more clearly Augustine's concept of free will, which I had first learned about in a course taught by Dr. Allers some eight years previously.

In the *Confessions*, Augustine presents an analysis of the will that stands us in good stead today. Augustine's thought is helpful when treating questions of sexual impurity and the human battle to avoid giving into these temptations. In our culture, we speak of someone with a strong will overcoming all kinds of obstacles on his way to success; on the other hand, we say that another person has a weak will, because he gives up too easily in a difficult task, or he is not able to resist temptations such as drinking, using drugs, or viewing pornography. But Augustine saw that what makes a will strong is found in one's motives for actions. Where the purposes and motive are *unified*, one acts with determination.

But when one's motives are mixed, when one feels torn between what one ought to do and what one desires to do—such as in the case in alcoholism, drug addiction, and lustful sexual desires—one vacillates between avoiding the act and giving in to it. On the pastoral level, this would lead to the person learning how to strengthen his good motives in order to develop a strong will.

I discussed this at length in my doctoral thesis, *The Moral Theology of the Confessions of Saint Augustine* (Catholic University of America, 1951). In the same volume I examined Augustine's analysis of bad habit as a chain taking away our freedom. Today, we would call such bad habits *addictions*.

One may discern four key links in this moral chain: (1) *perverse will*. This is found in the first deliberate act of impurity, which is primarily a rebellion of the spirit against the law of God. It is the basic "deordination" of the will from its greatest good, God, which gives rise to the consequent rebellion of the flesh against the spirit, and such disobedience to God's law opens the way for the next stage, namely, (2) *libido* or *perverted lust*. The initial pleasure of lust stimulates and excites the individual to seek the same pleasure again, and with repetition comes the third stage: (3) *consuetudo*, by which the soul is drawn powerfully to the vice it has sought frequently. Thus, an evil habit is formed from continued license; and such may be termed (4) *necessity*. Just as a chain is fashioned from the individual links, so is the will entangled by repeated acts of impurity until the individual believes that he must have the pleasure that comes from the activation of the addiction. Consequently, he despairs of his ability to resist its violence and yields to its impulses, as if unavoidable.

In summary, what Augustine called *necessity* is now described by psychologists as *addiction* or *compulsion*. You can see how freedom of the will decreases as the person gradually moves from one stage to another until he has lost freedom with regard to specific forms of sexual addictions—not only with illicit heterosexual and homosexual acts, but also the addictions to masturbation and pornography. This loss of freedom represents a loss of a great gift from God, namely, our ability to choose what is good.

Thus, as I developed my doctoral thesis, I was integrating pastoral moral theology with psychological insights from the study of the *Confessions*. I was able to draw together both the theological and psychological elements found in the topics of weakness of will and addictions. These were the exact comparisons and integrations I had sought to make some years before when I wanted to study psychology. The Lord does provide when we choose obedience. I also found in the *Confessions* a concept that I would develop over the next fifty years of my life—a concept I refer to as interior chastity or chastity of the heart.

THE LORD SETS THE DIRECTION

God has his mysterious ways. In 1953, I was teaching at De Sales School of Theology as well as at Dunbarton. Nine young priests, ordained at the end of their third year, wanted to have faculties to hear confessions during Holy Week which, that year, came at the end of March. In those days, all our newly-ordained priests had to pass a thirty-minute oral examination before being given the faculties to hear confession. This year, however, the provincial was sick, and in his absence a Scripture scholar and I prepared a written exam.

All the students passed, but I was called in by the provincial, Father William F. Buckley, who asked, "How come your students do not know much about homosexuality?" I was surprised at this question. The scriptural scholar had included two questions about homosexuality and the students did not do well on them. I explained that in my course plan, the issue of homosexuality did not come up in pastoral theology until some time in April, and that we would cover it next month. He replied, "OK, but make sure that next year's students know about homosexuality." I walked out of his office determined that next year's class would know about that issue and so, that summer, I spent many hours reading all the literature on it in Philadelphia's Logan Library.

Up to this time, the topic of homosexuality had been nothing more than a Latin footnote in the classical moral manuals. It was one of the subjects to be treated in pastoral theology, but just one among others, like alcoholism, drug addiction, and pornography.

After my reading of both psychological and spiritual authors on the subject, I was eager to write an article on the psychological aspects of the homosexual condition. I wanted priests to know something about it. Within a few months I had a rough draft which I shared with some fellow moralists and an editor. I received encouraging feedback and made revisions, but it was not published until I sent it to Father John Courtney Murray, S.J., then editor of the quarterly *Theological Studies*. Fr. Murray published the article in the March 1955 issue under the title "The Pastoral Problem of Homosexuality." When the article appeared, I received an immediate response from Jesuit missionaries throughout the world, many of them requesting reprints. I was happy that the article had been well received, but at the same time, I did not want to write about homosexuality again. Two years later, when Fr. John Ford, S.J., asked me why I had not written again on the subject, I admitted I didn't want to be known as the "homosexual priest." Fr. Ford encouraged me to continue writing on the subject. Because I had such esteem for him, I continued my research, which resulted in five published articles.

RENEWAL, REST, AND RE-CREATION

My studies in the area of homosexuality were clearly meeting a need in the Church. I continued my teaching and pastoral work, and by 1978 I began to give retreats to priests and brothers in perpetual vows who had experienced difficulties with same-sex attractions. These men were fearful that if anyone knew of their situation, they would be told to leave their diocese or religious order. The retreats were called "Renewal, Rest, and Re-Creation." I had begun this work because several years earlier a fellow Oblate, Fr. John Kenny, had challenged me to do it, even offering to raise the needed money for the idea. From 1978 to 1990 we averaged two retreats per year in the Diocese of Arlington, Virginia. Fr. Kenny was secretary-treasurer of our little enterprise and I gave the retreats. I was also ably assisted by Dr. John Kinnane, who taught at the Catholic University of America and was in private practice as a clinical psychologist. Once again, the Lord used someone else's prompting to bring out a good work through me.

As happened later in Courage, those who worked on the retreats and those who attended bound themselves to anonymity and confidentiality. I estimate about 250 priests and brothers made the retreats while I conducted them. I wrote about this program in *The Homosexual Person* (Ignatius Press, 1987). I was able to refer some of the priests and brothers to treatment centers where they would get further help. It was not an easy program; there were five days of rigorous self-examination and prayer. I worked with each participant personally, and I believe that most of them benefited from the experience. Sadly, the retreat program had little support from most of the bishops of that period, though Arlington's Bishop Thomas Welsh gave it warm support. When I was no longer able to conduct the retreats, I handed over the reins to a religious brother who continues the ministry today.

Those gatherings taught me the importance of group spirituality among members. I learned the powerful influence of group support in helping priests wounded with same-sex attraction who are striving to remain faithful to their promises and vows of chastity. I can see now that God was preparing me for something more.

Courage is Born

Aware of "Renewal, Rest, and Re-Creation," Fr. Benedict Groeschel (a Capuchin at the time) asked me to come to New York and discuss a similar group for Catholic lay men and women with same-sex attraction. Cardinal Cooke, the Archbishop of New York, had realized that Catholic men and women with same-sex attraction had no adequate guidance. The cardinal asked me to begin a support group and I readily agreed.

We formed the group in September 1980. Every Friday afternoon, I would come up from Washington to preside at this first gathering of five men and then meet with them individually afterwards. These men developed the five primary goals of Courage:[1]

1. *Chastity.* Live chaste lives in accordance with the Church's teaching on homosexuality.

2. *Prayer and Dedication.* Dedicate one's life to Christ through service to others, spiritual reading, prayer, meditation, individual spiritual direction, frequent attendance at Mass, and the frequent reception of the sacraments of Reconciliation and Holy Eucharist.

3. *Fellowship.* Foster a spirit of fellowship in which all may share thoughts and experiences, and so ensure that no one will have to face the problems of homosexuality alone.

4. *Support.* Be mindful of the truth that chaste friendships are not only possible but necessary in a chaste Christian life and in doing so provide

---

[1] For more information on the origins of Courage, I refer the reader to my books *The Homosexual Person* (Ignatius Press, 1987) and *The Truth about Homosexuality: the Cry of the Faithful* (Ignatius Press, 1996).

encouragement to one another in forming and
sustaining them.

5. *Good Example.* Live lives that may serve as good
   examples to others.

Early in the history of Courage, we ran into opposition from
a few members who were unable to make the distinction between
Courage and another group, Dignity. Courage emphasized
chastity. Dignity was vague about the issue at first, and later
took the position that same-sex acts between two persons could
be moral if there was fidelity and love—a position contrary to
authentic Catholic teaching. Later, at our 1990 annual conference
in Philadelphia, some visitors who were not Courage members
requested that Courage also strive to bring its members out of
the homosexual condition, a process known as *reparative therapy.*
It was suggested this could be the sixth goal. The members
rejected the idea. Many members who choose to lead a life of
chastity in the world do not feel the need for reparative therapy.
Courage encourages its members to seek psychological help
to move away from the condition but this is an option, not an
obligation. Courage now continues to stress the development of
meditation, a prayer life, interior chastity, and the formation of
chaste friendships as a protection of the gift of chastity.

In the latter part of my priestly ministry a considerable
portion of my time has been spent with the parents of persons
with same-sex attraction. They, too, need the help of the Church
as they strive to accept the permissive will of God, with all the
heartaches they experience in seeing one of their children in a
lifestyle contrary to the Gospel. The ministry within Courage
to help them—Encourage—began in 1990 in the Boston area,
and it has been a great support to parents and friends of those
struggling with same-sex attraction.

Despite its slow growth, due in large part to a massive
indifference on the part of many clergy and laity alike, Courage

has a clear program for the future. It aims to promote interior chastity—or chastity of the heart—within the Church. It stresses that each person must develop a life of prayer and interior chastity, supported by chaste friends.

Just before Christmas 2000, I became seriously ill with water on the lung, an irregular heartbeat, and bleeding ulcers. In most ways, I have recovered but have slowed down a bit. I now spend only three or four days a week on Courage concerns. My prayer for Courage at this time is that the Lord will provide a priest to assume the role of national leader. In the midst of our work, which at times seems daunting, I recall what Pope John Paul II said to David Morrison, one of our more well-known members: "Courage is doing the work of God." It is this conviction that keeps us going.

HUMILITY AND THE SALESIAN SPIRIT

As St. Francis de Sales lay on his deathbed, speechless from a stroke, the Visitation nuns asked him to write down the three most important virtues in their way of life. He wrote: "humility, humility, humility." Humility, the loving acceptance of one's limitations, joined to a trust that God gives us strength to carry out his will, is central to the Salesian way of life.

In the Salesian view, *what* you do is not as important as *how* you do it—the spirit with which you act. That is why St. Francis de Sales gave the Visitation Order and the Oblates of St. Francis de Sales a Spiritual Directory to guide one's prayer through the hours of the day and night, from morning prayer to night prayer. In part three of his Directory, St. Francis de Sales recommends that one direct the principal actions of the day to God, while accepting all the difficulties which one may encounter. Truly living the Spiritual Directory is more difficult than the performance of many external acts of penance. But once you begin this Directory life of prayer, you will want to hold on to it. As Oblates, we endeavor to use these interior acts of prayer in our daily ministry of Catholic education on every level, from grade school to university. The same spirit is found in parishes and missions where Oblates work. This spirit relies on a sense of humility.

I follow the Salesian spirit in my daily counseling sessions, at Courage meetings, in preaching on Sundays in parishes, and in responding to critics of the Courage and Encourage ways of life. In brief, I strive to exercise my priesthood in imitation of St. Francis de Sales.

In stressing the need which every priest, whether diocesan or religious, has for an interior life of prayer, I certainly do not intend to minimize the value of our external activities. All priests have very significant external acts to perform every day. The most important is the administration of all the sacraments save holy orders, which is ordinarily reserved to bishops. In the writings of St. Francis de Sales, however, the most important act that a priest performs is the offering of Jesus in the Holy Sacrifice of the Mass. Each day centers around the Mass, either in preparing for it from the evening before (hence, in the past, the observance of *le grand silence*), or in offering thanks to the Holy Trinity at the end of Mass.

At my ordination in 1944, I resolved that I would say Mass every day, as long as my health allowed. I have often been asked, "Father, does a priest *have to* say Mass every day?" The answer is no. Only once was I asked—in 1947 by a ten-year-old girl— "Father, do you *like* to say Mass?" The answer is yes! Even in their sickness, some priests continue to say Mass every day.

The administration of the sacrament of Reconciliation, the anointing of the seriously ill, and the confirming of converts are all actions in which the priest acts *in persona Christi*, in the person of Christ. Those who aspire to the priesthood should ask themselves whether they are willing to act in Christ's place in administering the sacraments. Pope John Paul II biographer George Weigel put it very accurately: a priest is an icon of Christ.

This is his identity, not whether he is an administrator of an apostolate, or chaplain to the New York Yankees, or a brilliant canon lawyer. I remember autographing one of my books for a Vatican archbishop who said, "Address it 'Father.' 'Father' is my most important title."

A WORD TO ASPIRANTS TO THE PRIESTHOOD

I would say to aspirants to the priesthood, whether they seek to be diocesan or religious order priests, should put aside personal ambition and seek only to follow Christ in the mission of the religious order or in the work of the diocese. Allow those in authority to direct you to the work of Christ, as it is discerned by the bishop or religious order superior. This does not mean that you become passive; there is plenty of room for creative approaches in the varied ministries of the Church.

At the present moment the Church is suffering from an over-reaction to the recent sexual abuse scandals. Some have held that the mere presence of same sex-attraction in a man is sufficient reason to exclude him from a religious order or a diocesan seminary. I do not believe that the Vatican will accept this view. From my fifty years of experience in counseling priests and laity, I know many priests and laity with same sex-attraction who lead chaste lives. For aspirants to priesthood and religious life, I propose another reflection on interior chastity.

In our contemporary culture, with its seductive images of sexuality and its reduction of the marital act to an instrument of physical ecstasy, it is difficult for those who believe in the virtue of chastity to avoid the fantasies of pleasure constantly thrust at them in the media. It is understandable that one who seeks to lead a chaste life may find himself battling sexual fantasies. Such a person may find himself drawn towards physical sex but refuse to give in. By the grace of God he remains chaste but with much torment. This may be described as "white-knuckle chastity," the imperfect virtue St. Thomas Aquinas refers to as *continence*.

As one learns to pray with the heart by daily meditation, though, one finds it easier to resist lust. Notice I did not say *easy*, but *easier*. The regular habit of mental prayer strengthens the motives for chastity, gradually purifying the heart and leading the individual to see chastity as another form of love of God. One may say that prayer of the heart leads to chastity of the heart, to a personal love of Jesus Christ. At this point in one's spiritual development, one seeks friends who also are chaste out of love for Christ. Such friendships help to preserve the chastity of the two friends or of the group of friends.

It is the work of the Holy Spirit that has guided the choices I made in entering a religious community. Of course, the Holy Spirit often worked mysteriously in my vocation, and I am sure there were times I followed Him without my knowing it. I thank Him for the guidance which He gave me, particularly through others. Only through the promptings of the Spirit can one be called to religious life and the priesthood. I say to those aspiring to either: Open your hearts to the Holy Spirit!

❧

11

An Openness to the Lord

Monsignor Charles M. Mangan

"I want to be gods like those people up there."

Those were my words to my mother at the age of four, while watching the priests in the sanctuary at Mass. Eventually, I learned that they weren't gods but God's own priests. And I wanted to be one of them. How humbling it is for me now to see that not only would I become a priest but that I would be called to serve two popes in Rome. I marvel at the ways of God—how he calls the unequipped but then equips them for the call.

I was born into a Catholic family in 1962, in Madison, Minnesota, the second of six children to Joseph and Gertrude (Martin) Mangan. Praying and attending Mass were a natural part of our family life. There was grace before and after meals and evening prayers every night. For prayers, we ran through a list my mother devised to which, as we got older, a decade of the Rosary was added. Mom also had holy water, which she sprinkled on us at night. And she was quick to pull it out and light blessed candles when a thunderstorm came our way.

In 1964, our family moved to Aberdeen, South Dakota, where Sacred Heart became our parish and grade school. I have many happy memories of the nuns who taught there—the Sisters of the Presentation of the Blessed Virgin Mary—and of the diocesan priests who staffed the parish. Having religion class every day and enjoying the sacramental opportunities in a Catholic school, I increasingly thought of the priesthood.

In the summer of 1972, two years after receiving my first holy communion, Sr. M. George Jurgens, P.B.V.M., trained me to be an altar boy. After that, Mom would take my older brother Tony and me to church every morning for the 6:45 Mass. Although I was a little tired at that hour, I loved serving. The candles, incense, and sacred vessels held a special allure for me. Soon the parish priests were calling the Mangan boys to serve weddings and funerals, too. Dad and Mom always said yes on our behalf which—except for a few Saturday afternoons when a ballgame beckoned—was OK with us.

In the fifth grade, the inevitable question arose: "What do you want to be when you grow up?" I answered without delay: "A priest." The sisters and our lay teachers were supportive of my reply, while my classmates were amused and a little disbelieving. I didn't mind. Just as praying at home with my family seemed natural, so did the prospect of the priesthood. My parents were pleased when I mentioned what I had told my class. It probably didn't seem unusual to them that one of their four sons wanted to become a priest. My father, who passed away in 2006, provided a tremendous example of humility and devout prayer. With my mother, he provided both spiritually and financially for us. I eagerly anticipate the day when I will see him anew in the kingdom of heaven!

As the years rolled by, I continued to think about the priesthood. I was confirmed in 1976 by Bishop Lambert A. Hoch of Sioux Falls. Dad was a native of Bishop Hoch's hometown of Elkton, South Dakota, so I always felt a special kinship to this towering prelate who died in 1990. That August of 1976, I entered Roncalli High School—named for Angelo Cardinal Roncalli, who would become Pope John XXIII (1958–1963). I continued to serve Mass in the parish and began to serve as lector during weekly Mass at school. My reading included Catholic newspapers, pamphlets from the rack in the back of church, and Catholic books that my parents had at home.

Little Did I Know...

As were so many worldwide, I was intrigued by the election of Karol Cardinal Wojtyla as the Vicar of Christ on October 16, 1978. As a junior in high school, I never would have guessed that Pope John Paul II would have such a big impact on my life and that one-day I would be working for him as a priest and member of his Roman Curia.

Just before Christmas of 1978, Sioux Falls' new bishop, Paul V. Dudley (who passed away in 2006), came to our school to celebrate Mass. When our school counselor, Sr. M. Pauline Quinn, P.B.V.M., told him that I wanted to be a priest, Bishop Dudley, with his characteristic warm smile, expressed his delight. From that day forward, despite the innumerable concerns he had as the shepherd of more than 100,000 Catholics, he never forgot my interest in the priesthood.

During my senior year, I spoke with our new priest-principal about my possible vocation and he was very encouraging. But instead of suggesting that I enter the seminary that Fall, he recommended that I attend the state college in town and live with my family for another four years. His reasoning was that, because I needed a college degree to be admitted to the major seminary, I could obtain one while being at home. He added that I could become involved in the local Aquinas Newman Center to maintain my interest in the priesthood.

Fifteen years later, when that priest and I reminisced about this discussion, he remained convinced it was good advice. I would hesitate before suggesting the same to an eighteen-year-old who showed every indication of desiring the priesthood, given that secular colleges often—if not always—pose considerable obstacles for those striving to be upright Catholics. Still, one cannot help but be amazed at how God works.

That fall I enrolled at Northern State College, two miles from home, to study music education. I had good teachers and was doing well in my classes, but my desire for the priesthood only increased. During the summer of 1982, between my sophomore and junior years, I felt an unrest deep within me. It was almost as if I suddenly needed to be a priest. I did not want to wait any longer! That July, I learned a lot about patience and perseverance. Though I was anxious to pursue my vocation, my decision to become a priest brought great tranquility. I knew that this was what God wanted for me.

By the time I graduated in May 1984 with a bachelor's degree in music education, I had already spoken with Bishop Dudley about entering the seminary that fall. He accepted me as a seminarian for the Diocese of Sioux Falls and chose to send me to Immaculate Heart of Mary Seminary in Winona, Minnesota. There was a program there for students like me, graduates of secular colleges who needed some philosophy classes before beginning theological studies in a major seminary.

FROM SEMINARY (AND SEMINARY) TO PRIESTHOOD

After a brief period of wondering whether I could really be a seminarian and some assurance from my Mom, I entered the seminary in the fall of 1984. My Dad also thought that I should give the seminary a try because I had expressed my desire to become a priest for many years—though he cautioned me several times to make sure that I was entering for the "right" reasons and not to please him and my Mom. So I left home. Although I missed my family, I enjoyed the peace of knowing that this was where the Lord wanted me to be.

I also began to understand that the seminary is an excellent place to discern one's vocation. A young lady with whom I had attended college once told me that she thought a man who had been to the seminary and then concluded that the priesthood was not his vocation would make a good husband because he had been formed in prayer and discernment. There is no shame for a man to enter the seminary and then, after having spent himself in prayer and in fulfilling the requirements of the school, discover with the assistance of spiritual direction and his bishop that the Lord is not calling him to the priesthood. Several men who arrived at Immaculate Heart of Mary Seminary the same day as I did gradually learned that their vocation lay elsewhere.

My year in Winona went quickly. The following spring, Bishop Dudley informed me that I would be going to Saint Paul Seminary in Saint Paul, Minnesota. I had heard that "SPS" had been having some problems, but I trusted my bishop and went forward. In August 1985, I entered Saint Paul's and, although I found the faculty and seminarians cordial, I sensed that something was missing, most notably a deep spirituality and an obedience to the pastors of the Church. In spite of that, I considered it to be a grace from God to have spent a year there. I understand that many changes have enriched this seminary since then.

During my year at SPS, I began to deepen in love for Jesus—the great High Priest—his Ever-Virgin Mother, Saint Joseph, and the angels and saints. I have always enjoyed reading about the saints—their heavenly intercession and stellar example have been a great comfort for me. To know that the Lord was in my corner, that I hadn't chosen Him but rather that He had chosen me, was a consolation—especially when I experienced my own weakness in responding to His love. And with the assistance of His Mother and our friends in Paradise, I knew that I could persevere.

After hearing my impression of the seminary and my willingness to remain if he so desired, Bishop Dudley decided to send me to Mount Saint Mary's Seminary in Emmitsburg, Maryland. I arrived on the Memorial of the Queenship of Mary, August 22, 1986.

Those three years at the "Mount" were life-changing. The world of moral and systematic theology, canon law, Mariology, and the Fathers of the Church was opened up to me as never before. I spent a lot of time preparing for examinations. Spiritually, I continued the daily practice that I had started in Winona of praying for a continuous hour in the presence of the Blessed Sacrament. The examples of four persons were particularly instrumental in this regard: Fr. Glenn F. Latterell, a priest I met while I was in college; Archbishop Fulton J. Sheen; Bishop Dudley; and Fr. Anthony J. Manochio, my spiritual director at the Mount.

I was grateful for the joyfulness of the faculty and the seminarians. We had as many as six men studying for the Diocese of Sioux Falls at one time. The apostolic work I was assigned to at the Mount was invaluable. I participated in visiting prisoners, attending sessions for those in a chemical dependency program, and helping Monsignor Hugh Phillips at the National Shrine of Our Lady of Lourdes just atop a hill overlooking the Mount. I had my first taste of the Legion of Mary there and immediately appreciated it as an evangelization effort from which any parish would obtain abundant fruit.

During my seminary years, I realized more than ever the debt of gratitude I owed so many for helping me on the way to the priesthood. My parents and siblings often formed me before I was even aware of it. And the fine Sisters of the Presentation of the Blessed Virgin Mary were also instrumental in my formation. Sr. M. Helen Freimuth, who taught me English in high school, always had a kind word. Her prayerfulness, sincerity, and charity toward others were a powerful witness that I have never forgotten. Frs. John Kasch and Joseph Murphy were two of my pastors as a youth. Their reverence during Mass made a profound impact on me. Even now, when celebrating Mass, I strive to exhibit the same devotion they had at the altar. The witness of two priests and the Sister Helen made me want to emulate those same qualities in my own vocation.

As Fr. Manochio has said, "as a seminarian, so as a priest." This is not to deny the possibility of divine grace stirring up a priest who perhaps was not a diligent seminarian. Nor does this negate the fact that, sadly, a pious seminarian could later become a mediocre priest due to a lack of effort and cooperation with God's grace. Fr. Manochio's comment impressed upon me the need to be vigilant and to use my time well. This advice, it seems to me, is good for anyone regardless of vocation. One can either develop or regress as a disciple of Jesus.

Priestly celibacy was a topic we often discussed in the seminary. Many today doubt—or even deny—its importance. My beliefs on celibacy as a priest remain the same as when I was a seminarian: the Church is very wise to require this charism of her priests. Why? It is not to say that marriage is a defective vocation, to be lived by those who "can't hack celibacy." Rather, the Church requires celibacy because it demonstrates loudly that one is trying to live with his eyes fixed on another realm— heaven—in which people "aren't given or taken in marriage" (see Luke 20:34). When we look at a Catholic priest, we should see "another Christ," someone who—though imperfect—is doing his best to raise our minds and hearts to heaven. Celibacy is a vehicle by which this can happen. It is, as well, a living out here on earth of the heavenly marriage to the Trinity that all of the saved will experience in heaven. As celibates, we priests are both witnesses to this eschatological reality and participants in it in time.

The grace to be celibate comes from God himself. The Church expects her priests to possess this charism. For me, celibacy is a liberating experience. It frees me to commit myself wholly to Christ and to live entirely for His Church without concern about family responsibilities. In the seminary, I knew that some seminarians struggled with whether they had been granted the charism of celibacy. I think that I was spared this trial. I had known for many years that my God-given vocation was to the priesthood, so the prospect of celibacy was not a trial for me. My recommendation to seminarians or those discerning the priesthood is to pray for wisdom on this specific question.

My three years at Mount Saint Mary's Seminary flew by. I was ordained to the diaconate on Sunday, May 29, 1988, the Solemnity of the Holy Trinity, and, thirteen months later, on June 29, 1989, the Solemnity of Sts. Peter and Paul, three other men and I were ordained to the priesthood by Bishop Dudley in St.

Joseph's Cathedral in Sioux Falls. Forty-five minutes before our ordination, the bishop told the four of us that he marveled at how different each of us was from the other three yet God had called each of us to the same reality: the holy priesthood of Jesus Christ.

FROM SIOUX FALLS TO ROME

The day after my ordination, I celebrated a Mass of Thanksgiving at my home parish, Sacred Heart, in Aberdeen. Though it was another blistering day, I do not recall minding. I offered the Votive Mass of the Sacred Heart of Jesus, and I was grateful for the presence of all the priests, religious, and faithful who attended. I remember being quite nervous before the Mass and hoping that I would do everything correctly. I recall the moment of consecration and thinking how Jesus had given me the power to change bread and wine into His body and blood. After the Mass, a prie-dieu was set up in the gymnasium of the parish school for me to give my first blessing to all who approached.

My first assignment was as parochial vicar at St. Joseph Cathedral in Sioux Falls. Bishop Dudley once remarked that spending a year at the cathedral was like spending two in another parish, given the magnitude and abundance of the work! I taught in the parish school and in the religious education program for the public school students once a week. I heard confessions four times a week, conducted a weekly holy hour, visited the hospital once a week, and visited those in the nursing home and took Holy Communion to the shut-ins monthly. During those years I prepared hundreds of persons for marriage and baptism, counseled both parishioners and those who knocked at the rectory door, and so on. Of course, I celebrated Mass daily and several times on Sundays. Offering the Holy Sacrifice of the Mass was—and remains—the highlight of my day. It was a thrilling time for me. I loved the priesthood and was glad that Jesus had selected me to share it with Him. There was nothing else that I would rather have done.

My first three years as a priest went rapidly. In the spring of 1992, Bishop Dudley said he needed to send one of his priests to study canon law and decided that I would go to Rome. I had never been to the Eternal City, and I was somewhat intimidated by the possibility. But I arrived there that July and began studying Italian in preparation for enrolling in one of the pontifical universities.

I spent two years in Rome, living at the graduate house of the Pontifical North American College (called the Casa Santa Maria dell'Umiltà) with seventy other diocesan priests from the United States. I obtained a licentiate in canon law from the Pontifical Gregorian University, but I think I learned more outside the classroom than in it. Another culture, another language, another people. To pray at the tombs of the martyrs, to visit the four major basilicas and so many other churches besides, to attend the papal liturgies and see Pope John Paul II up-close, to learn from my brother priests at the Casa. I treasured those days, realizing that soon I would be home again to apply what I had received. What a blessing to be in Rome! I couldn't thank Bishop Dudley enough for opening up a new world to me.

During my final year in Rome, Bishop Robert J. Carlson (then auxiliary bishop of Saint Paul and Minneapolis) was appointed the coadjutor bishop of Sioux Falls. I had met Bishop Carlson some years before and knew his reputation as a bishop fully in communion with the Holy Father. Bishop Carlson sent me a letter that spring saying I would be assigned as vice-chancellor of the diocese, defender of the bond in the tribunal, and pastor of two rural parishes. I returned home in June 1994 and, for the next four years, was involved in both diocesan and parochial work. I was very grateful for all the opportunities to serve in both areas.

Because Pope John Paul II spent so much energy inviting the faithful throughout the world to reflect on the Blessed Mother and her relationship to the friends of her Son, Bishop

Carlson was convinced the diocese should have a priest trained in Mariology. So, in September 1998, he sent me back to Rome to study at the Pontifical Theological Faculty Marianum. Again, a new horizon appeared. To ponder and analyze all that Mary is for us is an exercise in thankfulness and awe. She cheerfully and infallibly leads us to her divine Son, aiding us to become better disciples of the God-Man. Our Lady has great love for her priest-sons, given their likeness to her own Son. We priests have a grave obligation to transmit Christ to the world. Whom should we emulate more than Mary? Her burning desire was to share Jesus with everyone. That is to be the wish of every priest.

Being in Rome for the Great Jubilee of the Year 2000 was a spiritual treat. I attended the opening of the holy doors at three of the four major basilicas, participated in numerous papal ceremonies and audiences, and met many pilgrims from around the globe. Even more than usual, Rome became alive with action that reminded us—on the two-thousandth anniversary of Jesus' birth—of the splendor of the Almighty, his benevolence, and his overwhelming mercy towards his needy sons and daughters.

Toward the end of that year, I received a great surprise. Every so often, bishops are asked to release one of their priests to work in the Roman Curia. Bishop Carlson informed me of my new assignment: to be an official in the Vatican Congregation for Institutes of Consecrated Life and Societies of Apostolic Life. This dicastery is the Holy Father's arm in reaching out to those who are members of religious institutes, secular institutes, and societies of apostolic life.

I began this pastoral work on January 8, 2001—two days after the Great Jubilee concluded. It is a joy for me to assist in some small way members of religious institutes, secular institutes and societies of apostolic life, consecrated virgins and hermits. I can only marvel at seeing how the Holy Spirit is working in the lives of these persons. Not only do they draw closer to Christ but they also inspire *all* members of the Church, regardless of personal vocation, to do likewise.

On November 19, 2003, Pope John Paul II named me a chaplain of his holiness, which carries the title "monsignor." This is considered by many to be a honor, a recognition of past service to the Holy Father and the Church. But I look at it as a responsibility—a new opportunity to recommit myself to care for the Body of Christ without any desire for special acknowledgment. In the world, power and authority are pursued with a vengence. Sadly, this can even be the case in the Church. Titles take on great importance in the minds of some. Although I fully believe that all authority is ultimately from God—and actually a foreshadowing of the Fatherhood of God—I have come to believe the older I get that authority and honor is given to people precisely so they can become better servants of others rather than be served by others.

Three recent occurrences within a brief span provided me with ample reason to be grateful anew. On October 14, 2006, at the age of seventy-eight, my dad passed to Everlasting Life. Five weeks later, Bishop Dudley, a week shy of his eightieth birthday, was also called by God. I will never be able to thank the Lord sufficiently for my dad and Bishop Dudley, two true fathers in the mode of the Eternal Father who I pray have already heard those immortal words spoken by Jesus Christ that each of us should anticipate with all his heart: "Come, you who are blessed by My Father. Inherit the kingdom prepared for you from the foundation of the world" (Matthew 25:34). The Holy Spirit tempered my sadness by providing a new bishop for my Diocese upon the transfer of Bishop Carlson to the Diocese of Saginaw. Bishop Paul Joseph Swain was ordained to the Episcopate on October 26, 2006 as the eight bishop of the Diocese of Sioux Falls. This gentle shepherd brings fresh vitality to fortify the legacy of faith, hope and charity left by his predecessors.

Happy Catholic, Happy Priest

Having been a priest for some eighteen years, I readily admit my weakness but also confess my trust in the Lord. He has been the mainstay throughout my life but especially as his priest. I often thank God for the teachings of His Church. The doctrines of the Catholic Church are systematic and persuasive; they have brought solace and enlightenment to its members for two thousand years.

These teachings have helped me in my own spiritual and intellectual development. If I am in any sense a follower of Christ, it is due to his unparalleled grace and the mind-opening and soul-stirring doctrines of the Church. I am fascinated by the truths that the Church presents regarding God, the human person, and the obligations that man has towards his neighbor. The Church's teachings have challenged me to see God, not me, as the center of the universe and to note that my responsibilities to my fellow human beings are real and substantial.

Sometimes the Church's doctrines are criticized, often by influential individuals or the secular press. It is said that the Church's teachings are out of touch with the twenty-first century. In many ways, they are! But it does not follow that our modern age is right and the Church is wrong. Far from being steeped in wisdom, our contemporary culture lacks insights into the realities of God and the next life. Instant gratification has become dominant. No wonder the Church—in line with the Gospel—is considered "not with the times." Ratcheting up the ante a bit on this topic, I would even say the Church's teachings are desperately needed by today's culture, which is swimming in a sea of relativism that is, in many ways, the cause of so many of our problems. In many ways, it is these very teachings that are (and will continue) to hold much of the culture together. Contrary to popular belief, the teachings of the Church are not a shackle but a life-giving tether to the source of all truth, goodness, and beauty—God himself.

TIME WITH JESUS

As a priest, I am constantly buoyed by my reception and administration of the sacraments. To offer Mass daily and to hear confessions has been a tremendous solace for me. I have seen lives changed by the sacraments. And, through no worthiness of my own, I know that my life and the lives of others have been transformed positively because of my connection to the sacraments of penance and the most holy Eucharist.

I have been edified by watching my brother priests increase in their personal sanctity. Although numerous factors are involved, I believe a daily holy hour in the presence of the most Blessed Sacrament plays the most important role in one's growth in holiness. This link with Jesus in the Eucharist is a sure path to being more conformed to him. It is where vocations are found and sustained. It has been said that one cannot draw closer to Christ and remain the same.

Who can count all the gifts of being Catholic? The sacramental life available to us is beyond belief. One of my continuing challenges as a priest is to convey the marvelous and efficacious treasures we possess: the sacraments, our Blessed Lady and the papacy, to name just three.

I am amazed at how many Catholic laity genuinely love their Church. And I sense their pain when some sadness intervenes or when a scandal rears its ugly head. Two cases come to mind. First, in my predominantly rural Diocese of Sioux Falls, those who live in the areas of lesser population realize that priests are stretched thin. Some priests have two or three parishes simultaneously. I had three years in parish ministry when I covered two parishes, and one year working at three. There is sorrow and dismay among many people when they realize that their parish may be closed.

Second, the very grave sin of sexual abuse against children that has been committed by a tiny fraction of priests has caused heartache for Catholics in the United States and around the world. Through the mercy of God and the cooperation of those in authority in the Church, may terrible plague be eradicated soon.

The shortage of priests in various parts of the world and the scandal of sexual abuse by clergy may delay the new springtime in the Church called for by Pope John Paul II. However, these two realities will not cancel the age of fresh promise that is on the horizon. Jesus has not abandoned His Church. If anything, we have abandoned Him.

If I had a thousand lives to live, I would desire to be a priest again in each. There is nothing else that attracts me; there is nothing else I would rather do. I am content and grateful as a priest of Jesus Christ, despite my personal sin and unworthiness. My advice to a young man discerning the priesthood or consecrated religious life, or a young lady contemplating the consecrated religious life is this: turn to the Most Sacred Heart of Jesus, the Immaculate Heart of Mary and Saint Joseph. Your friendship with the Son, his Mother and the patron of the Church will allow you to hear the Holy Spirit whisper what the Father desires of you. You will never regret your openness to the Lord.

ﻼ

12

MY HEROES HAVE ALWAYS BEEN COWBOYS: HOW I BECAME A JESUIT PRIEST

FR. MITCH PACWA, S.J.

By the time I was five years old I knew *exactly* what I wanted to be—a cowboy. I would spend hours playing with sets of plastic cowboys, soldiers, and Indians, and I loved pretending to be a wrangler or a pony soldier as I rode my bike through the neighborhood. Cowboy shows were my favorite television programs and I devotedly headed to the local theater on Saturdays to watch westerns.

Still, despite repeated requests on birthdays and at Christmas, my hoped-for pony never materialized. My parents' finances were limited, as was the space in the small house trailer we called home.

My parents, Mitchell Pacwa and Lorraine Szczerba, were married in Chicago on October 2, 1948, and I was born nine-and-a-half months later. Both my parents' families were Polish and Catholic. While the Pacwas did not practice their faith much—some had even abandoned it—the Szczerbas went to Mass every Sunday, prayed often, and believed more strongly. When I was growing up, we were always members of the local parish, but our attendance at Sunday Mass was erratic. When we did go, it was Mom who took us. Dad would come along on Christmas and Easter.

My father had doubts about the faith, sometimes wondering whether it was all a hoax. He had been deeply affected by the evils of war, some of which he had seen firsthand while stationed in Africa during World War II. He questioned why God allowed such things as wars, but he admitted feeling divine intervention in preserving his life from sickness and danger during his time overseas. Later, he prayed for us and the needs of our family. (I have two brothers and one sister.) Dad worked long, hard hours, scrambling to keep us housed, clothed, and fed. Like so many of his contemporaries, he *never* wanted us to be as hungry and poor as his family had been during the Great Depression. His search for a better life took us to Miami in 1952, where he worked on betting machines for race tracks in Florida and around the country.

Three years later, we headed for Colorado Springs, Colorado, with Dad driving a truck loaded with gambling devices to be delivered to the local dog track and Mom driving the family car towing our still-horseless house trailer.

We were pleased to discover Colorado Springs was a small city, beautifully set below Pikes Peak within earshot of the loud echoes of thunder in the rock formation known as the Garden of the Gods. While this heaven of mountain horse trails, ghost towns, and beautiful vistas never included my own pony, I did get my first pair of cowboy boots for my sixth birthday and I *loved* them!

In 1957, Dad's company wanted him to make a six-month stay in Canada without his family. Instead, he quit his job and took us back to our old hometown of Chicago. For the next twelve years, he drove trucks and cabs, worked as a mechanic, and sold cars. Our time there gave us kids the chance to become better acquainted with our grandparents, great-grandparents, aunts and uncles.

This was the first time we attended a Catholic school, St. Priscilla's on Chicago's Northwest side. Being close to my mom's more religious family and attending Catholic school introduced me to a culture more thoroughly permeated by Catholic practices and ways of thinking. The Franciscan Sisters of Our Lady of Lourdes not only showed wonderful care educating us on basic subjects but also managed to include religious practices into the rhythm of the school day.

I was in the third grade when we returned to Chicago, but since I had not yet made my First Holy Communion, I joined the second-graders for their preparation classes. I still remember Sr. Saul teaching us about the importance of inviting Jesus into our hearts, about the need to spend time talking to him as to a friend, and about preparing our hearts by asking God to forgive our sins. She told us stories of St. Tarcissus and St. Dominic Savio to show us how much little children can love our Lord in the Blessed Sacrament. Very earnestly, the second-graders and I went to first confession and received First Holy Communion on Mothers' Day, May 11, 1958.

It was right around this time that I started to rein in my career plans to be a cowboy. Despite the allure of ropin' and ridin', I began to think that I might want to be a priest. Certainly, I was impressed by the fine priests and nuns at St. Priscilla's Parish who stimulated my interest in a religious vocation. Though the public school teachers had always been very good to us, it seemed that the Sisters and Fathers loved us and took great care to make sure we went to heaven. Though I still felt attracted to the cowboys who knew right from wrong, stood up for the weak, had exciting adventures, took risks to help people, and rode horses everywhere, I began to see that priests did some of the same good deeds, though none of them had horses. I transferred my dreams of being a cowboy to ideas of being a priest—maybe I could even be a cowboy chaplain!

"Sneaking" into the Seminary

When I was about eleven, my grandparents on my mother's side, "Busia" and "Dziadziu" to a Polish child, took me to Sunday Mass at the Divine Word Seminary in Techny, Illinois. At the gift shop, a member of that order gave me a form to join the "Future Priests Club." Membership included receiving a monthly magazine—the first mail I ever got. The stories of the missions and the priests' work in other countries led me to consider serving the Church overseas, which certainly entailed adventure and the possibility of riding a motorcycle instead of a horse.

Those articles brought back to my mind a story in my fourth-grade geography book that had truly impressed me. This Catholic geography text related that after St. Francis Xavier and the early Jesuits had made many converts in Japan, Christianity came under persecution there. Before the missionaries were martyred, they told the Japanese Catholics that priests would someday return and they were to ask them three questions to make sure those newcomers *were* priests: Do they honor the pope as the head of the Church? Do they honor the Blessed Virgin? Do they marry?

Two hundred and fifty years later, when a missionary arrived in Nagasaki, the local Japanese Catholics asked him the three questions before coming to him for the sacraments. Thousands of Japanese Catholics followed. The long-lasting quality of the early Jesuits' missionary activity certainly impressed me.

I was twelve when my dad, now a used-car salesman, became concerned that my interest in the priesthood was serious. A bit frustrated, he asked me, "Why do you want to be a priest? You don't have to be a priest to help people. Why not be a doctor and help people?" I answered, "Dad, being a doctor is a good thing, and it would be good to heal people. However, later on, they will die anyway. If I am a priest and hear someone's confession before death, the person will live in heaven forever. It's a better deal!" He didn't know what to say to that, but he was not very happy.

I decided I wanted to attend a minor seminary for high school, but the cost of tuition made a boarding school out of the question. Fortunately, the Archdiocese of Chicago's minor seminary accepted day students and was only an hour bus ride from home. My father forbade me to take the entrance exam, but I sneaked out of the house with to go take the test anyway. I met with seven of my eighth-grade classmates St. Priscilla's parking lot so that a young assistant, Fr. Thomas Dore, could drive us to Quigley North Preparatory Seminary for the entrance exam.

Dad was on his way to drive the parish school bus for a Cub Scout outing when he saw me and stopped. It was clear he was angry that I was disobeying him, but because Fr. Dore was there, Dad didn't make a big scene. The young priest tried to ease the tension by suggesting, "Let the kid try it; what can you lose?" I passed the exam, was accepted at the school, and attended Quigley for four years. It took that long for my stomach to heal.

Named for Chicago's Archbishop James E. Quigley, the school had campuses on the north and south sides of town. My class at Quigley North had about two hundred and fifty boys when we began, and the south campus was about the same. From that group of more than five hundred students, thirty-eight were ordained to the priesthood: two Jesuits, a Benedictine, and thirty-five diocesan priests. (The ratio was typical. About ten percent of a freshman high school seminary class went all the way to ordination. As one seminary professor once pointed out, most had "a vocation to be a seminarian" for a while before answering God's call in another way.)

We received a terrific education. The curriculum offered only one elective course in four years. We could take a foreign language (in addition to Latin, of course!). I picked Polish. We had four years of Latin, English, history, religion, and music, with standard courses in mathematics and a chemistry class. My grades were unimpressive, and I ended up graduating in the lowest of the four groups in my class. I tried hard, but I passed math and chemistry only by the hair of my chinny-chin-chin, which was not a significant amount in those days. And when reading poetry and literature, I had no idea how the teacher or other students derived their insights. Despite a lackluster academic career, I loved Quigley and learned enough to eventually do well when I went to college.

It wasn't all academics at school. Part of the fun of attending the school was going downtown everyday. In my junior and senior years, I got a job delivering papers in the Loop (i.e., the downtown area of Chicago that is so-called because it is surrounded by a loop of elevated train tracks), where a walk through the bustling crowds and impressive buildings was a delight. Being in downtown Chicago opened windows to elements of culture that were not well known in my working-class neighborhood.

Quigley was also an excellent preparation for the spiritual life of a future priest. Every seminarian was required to attend Mass and pray a rosary daily, go to confession weekly, and help out at his local parish. (I served Mass and assisted counting the Sunday collection.) Each class had a spiritual director who offered weekly conferences on the spiritual life. We had a fine spiritual formation and support overall.

One oddity about our school was that we attended class on Saturday and had Thursday as a free day. This European model of a seminary schedule helped encourage us to obey one of the school rules—no dating. We were not allowed to attend dances or "mixed parties." Since we were in class on Saturday, much of the Friday night was spent doing homework instead of socializing.

My fellow seminarians and I often got together to play poker on Wednesday or Saturday night. (Now you know how some of the clergy get to be such card sharks.) Sometimes we went to the college seminary in Niles, a Chicago suburb, to play basketball, see a movie, or hang out with the students from our parish. This provided a social support system for our young vocations.

OFF TO WAR OR TO THE JESUITS

As much as I loved Quigley, I spotted a couple of "warning flags" which suggested I should consider the religious life instead of the diocesan priesthood.

The first had to do with money. Family finances were always a concern. Tuition at Quigley was low ($175 for the first two years and $200 for the last two), but it was still a burden on my parents' budget. Since Dad remained strongly opposed to me being a priest, the additional expense was even less welcome to him. I gladly helped out with my paper route and with a job on Saturdays after school. I worked as a busboy at Saranecki Brothers' Catering Hall. The pay was not good, but I didn't have many marketable skills and lacked the gumption to get a better job.

Instead, I tried to make my ninety cents an hour go farther by investing my wages in the stock market. For a few weeks I carefully watched the daily reports and then found a banker from the parish who was willing to act as my broker. I really enjoyed keeping track of the market and reading business reports. In junior year, I did a paper on the stock market for the school science fair and won second prize. I even organized a few other guys into an investors club to help them understand stocks.

But then I began to reconsider my fascination with finances. If I was so focused on that as a sixteen-year-old kid, what would I be like when I got older? Would I end up obsessed and begin to neglect my duties as a priest? Perhaps I didn't have the moral strength to avoid the temptation to avarice. Maybe a religious life, where private ownership was not allowed, would be a better choice for me because a religious takes a vow of poverty; a diocesan priest does not.

The second "warning flag" that had me reconsidering the diocesan priesthood was what was happening at the college seminary where my classmates and I went to play basketball. By the spring of 1966, some of the priests on its faculty were leading the seminarians in encounter groups instead of prayer. Only one priest spiritual director continued to teach the younger men in his study group to pray; those running the encounter groups emphasized the importance of psychological honesty and openness in sharing one's feelings and thoughts in the small group settings. Eventually, all but one of those priests left the priesthood. You can guess which one stayed. Clearly, we high school seminarians were receiving a better spiritual formation at Quigley than the guys were at the college seminary. This experience was key in my discerning the direction of my vocation.

A few days after Christmas of my junior year, these impressions solidified into a definitive idea that came to me with sudden and startling clarity: I will *not* be a diocesan priest. Three days later, I was rocked by another: I will be a Jesuit.

I had never even *met* a Jesuit; I knew nothing about the Society of Jesus except for my impression from that fourth-grade geography book and the story of St. Francis Xavier. Obviously, that small lesson still impressed me seven years later. I even began to consider the possibility of seeking work in the missions.

The next step was to move beyond my initial inspiration to a true discernment of God's will. Did the Lord *really* want me to continue in the archdiocesan seminary, become a Jesuit, or do something else? This period of thought and reflection took two-and-a-half years.

One of the first things I did was write to the Jesuit vocations director, Fr. Dennis Schmidt, S.J. He quickly sent information about the novitiate and the course of training for a Jesuit. He also included material on Jesuit saints and apostolates. Later, we met to discuss my call and the need to meet with a Jesuit priest about discernment.

I also talked to my parents at a very memorable dinner where I presented the two options I was considering. First, I told them I thought I might join the army to fight the communists in Vietnam. Would I have their permission? My veteran father's "no" was clear and final.

Well then, I was also considering joining the Jesuits. I can still see Dad turning to Mom and asking, "What the hell is he talking about this time?" As my mother explained about the society founded by St. Ignatius Loyola, my father became even more upset about my interest in the Jesuits than he had been about my becoming a diocesan priest. Finally, he turned back to me and said, "If you go through with this and become a Jesuit priest, you will be out of my will." It was the position he held for the next decade. It was also a source of great pain in my life since my desire to be a priest was my response to following Jesus rather than an attempt to displease my father. I truly hoped it would please him but my commitment to pursuit of the priesthood was a source of tension between us and sadness for me. He was more interested in having me present him with grandchildren—and he was afraid that I might not be able to make the commitment to lifelong celibacy. He preferred that I avoid failure to keep my vows which would bring embarrassment to myself and the family.

Back at Quigley, I mentioned my interest in the Jesuits to a priest on the faculty. He thought I should attend a Jesuit high school for my senior year, but I knew that my family could never afford it, even at 1966 prices. The closest school, Loyola Academy, was in the suburb of Wilmette and I would need a driver's license and a car to get there. In Chicago itself the bus and the trains were close at hand and cheap for students. How could my folks afford a tuition hike plus a car and insurance?

In my senior year the new archbishop, Cardinal Cody, changed Quigley's practice of holding classes on Saturday instead of Thursday. He also allowed us to attend dances and mixed parties and to date girls. I more than willingly accepted *that* new policy. I welcomed it with gusto! I *loved* attending high school dances with my neighborhood friends. I didn't date very often but I definitely enjoyed dances.

What would cause the strict seminary life to take this sudden turn? In those turbulent years right after Vatican II, some priests and bishops thought that the days of the celibate priesthood were numbered. This helped some conclude there was no longer any need to prepare seminarians for the celibate life.

My desire for the priesthood didn't wane; I simply was having a lot of fun. Throughout the year, my mother drove me to Loyola Academy in Wilmette to meet with various Jesuits who taught me more about the Society of Jesus and examined me as a candidate that spring. The examiners thought it best for me to wait a year and apply again after studying at a Jesuit university.

This postponement was something of a shock; I had so counted on entering the Jesuits that I hadn't even taken the SAT examinations to get into a college. I graduated from Quigley North Preparatory Seminary in May 1967 without a college acceptance or money for tuition.

That summer I had a job in the mail room at an insurance company on the outskirts of the city. (By now I had a motorcycle—a seventeen-year-old's equivalent to a five-year-old's pony.) That summer, I worked a few jobs, took the SAT exams, and applied to Chicago's Loyola University. Just a week before classes began I received my acceptance notice in the mail. At an initial interview on campus, the priest who served as the admissions office gave me a blunt assessment of my chances of success: "Your SAT results are OK, but your grades in high school are crap. Attending Loyola University would be a waste of our time and your money. Why not just go home?"

Somewhat stunned, I sheepishly explained that I would like to try anyway. He answered that he doubted I could make it, but shrugging, invited me to "come on and choose [my] classes."

FROM COLLEGE ROMANCE TO THE NOVITIATE

I was both embarrassed and angered by what the priest said because I knew he was right about my grades. It was that anger that motivated me to study hard enough to get a "B" average both semesters of freshman year.

I also began dating more. A cute girl in my Spanish class took the same train I did and soon we began visiting inside and outside of class. We became good friends and then ended up going out together for about six months.

I came *this close* to proposing in a movie theatre while we were watching a re-release of *Gone with the Wind.* Caught up in romance, I turned to her to pop the question but the words did not come out. I had recently begun the process of applying to the Jesuits for the second time. Before I said anything to her, I decided, "If I don't get accepted into the Society this time, then I'll take it as a sign that I should get married."

A few weeks later I received my acceptance letter with instructions on what to bring to the novitiate in Milford, Ohio. I felt so happy, but also foolish for asking God to give me a sign to show me to enter the Jesuits. I realized that more than a momentary desire is needed to accept a vocation from God. His call to the priesthood had been a steady theme for ten years of my short life. Even if that acceptance letter had never come, a proposal of marriage, regardless of how delightful the woman, surely required more than the passing thoughts I had given this other vocation. On August 21, 1969, my family drove me to Milford, Ohio, where the novitiate sat on the banks of the Little Miami River. Finally, I was going to become a Jesuit.

There was new novice master that year. Fr. Paul Robb, S.J. was a psychologist who introduced insights from his own background into our training. We were also taught Jesuit history and spirituality, and taking part in the work around the house, all of which served to bind each man more closely to the Society of Jesus.

The late 1960s were turbulent times throughout the Church in America. Our novitiate tucked away on the Little Miami River, Ohio did not escape the turmoil. We began with thirty-one men in the class but that number dropped steadily throughout the fall. In the thirty or so days between Thanksgiving and Christmas, seventeen men packed their bags and left. A classmate's leaving became so common that a custom developed: the fellow would tell the guys of his decision during a walk around the grounds. It wasn't easy to hear that message so many times in such a short period, since the commitment to my Jesuit vocation included a commitment to my brothers within the Society. Their departures did not make me question my vocation so much as make me wonder why they left, especially since they had so many talents to offer our Lord. Christmas was fairly grim that year for those of us who remained.

ALONE WITH GOD

We first-year novices began our thirty-day private retreat right after New Year's Day. This was the first directed "long retreat" in the novitiate's history and a welcome blessing to me. Previously, it had been preached to the group as a whole and the master of novices had met one-on-one with individuals infrequently because of the large numbers with which he was dealing.

That was not a problem with my class. By now, there were only eight of us. The novice master met with each of us each day, directing us to the proper meditations as the Holy Spirit encountered each man at the level that man could reach. There was no talking among ourselves, except for the two-and-a-half "break days" St. Ignatius had worked into the structure of the retreat. Amazingly, our class bonded more closely in those four weeks of silence than in the previous four months of everyday living together.

For thirty days, I would be alone with God, fully engaged to and ready to hear his voice and follow his direction. Those thirty days helped me better learn the power of silently drawing toward God the Father through our Lord Jesus Christ in the power of the Holy Spirit and with the intercession of the Blessed Virgin Mary. St. Ignatius set up the meditations so as to incorporate a very personalized relationship with the Persons of the Blessed Trinity and with the Virgin Mary, these personal elements into his method of prayer throughout the *Spiritual Exercises* while at the same time leading the retreatant through four stages (the four weeks of the *Exercises*) of spiritual growth.

The first week of the *Spiritual Exercises* focuses on the need for the sinner to approach Jesus Christ with a thoroughly honest examination of life. My earlier instincts had been to think that God would love me if I were a good guy. I feared owning up to my sins and I preferred to claim that they were a result of my environment, family or when I could blame no one else. During the retreat, the meditations on the history of human sin from Adam to the present helped me realize that I had to take full responsibility for my own wrongdoing. I dreaded to admit my responsibility, fearing God's rejection of me. However, because St. Ignatius instructed retreatants to take their sinfulness to Jesus Christ on the cross, I learned that he died precisely to forgive these sins.

What amazed me was that the more honest I could be before our Lord in confessing my sins, the greater peace I felt. No longer was "Jesus loves sinners" simply words. This was a powerful experience which affected not only the way I go to confession but the way I hear them. I am a fellow sinner who has been chosen by Christ as an instrument to absolve sins. My task is to help others accept their responsibility for their own sinful actions, not to rub their face in the evil of sin but to open them to the realization that Christ truly died for them, loves them, and reconciles them to the Father.

An additional spiritual fruit came at the end of that first week, a time when St. Ignatius asks retreatants to meditate on Christ the King. I began to understand better that Jesus Christ accepted poverty and humility within human history in order to win souls from the power of sin and Satan. Our Lord invites each of us to join him, while at the same time Satan and his wicked angels are seeking recruits to aid in the temptation of the world. Knowing myself as a sinner who is loved to the death by Jesus Christ gave me a freedom to offer myself to be whatever the Lord wanted me to be. The specific vocation—Jesuit priest or brother, diocesan priest, husband and father of a family, or single layman—no longer mattered because I knew that Christ loved me so much that *anything* He wanted for me would be the best thing for me.

In a moment of prayer, I experienced a flash of light in my mind that I was truly called to be a Jesuit priest. That has been the touchstone experience which has sustained my vocation since my joining the Society of Jesus in 1968 and my ordination in 1976.

For the man discerning the priesthood, the first week of the *Exercises* offers the opportunity to see more clearly that he is a sinner in need of Christ's redemption; he is not so holy so as to be beyond the experience of sin which affects the rest of humanity. Furthermore, reflecting on his sin helps him discern the different influences in his life—those which would lead him away from Christ through sin, those which would draw him closer to Christ. Such discernment makes it easier to differentiate among the interior movements of the Holy Spirit which might be drawing him to the vocation the Lord has chosen for him. For the ordained priests, the *Exercises* not only help them with the tasks of the first week mentioned above, but they go on to meditate upon the life of Christ. The second week is filled with meditations on Christ's public life; the third week concerns His passion and death; the fourth week centers on His resurrection. By coming to know Christ more intimately through meditation on His life, priests can learn better to model their lives and their ministries on Jesus Christ, to whom the priesthood most truly belongs as its source and goal.

This key experience did not mean that my life always went smoothly for the rest of my first year in the novitiate or during all that followed. Many difficulties occurred due to my own sins, my limited abilities, my foolishness and naiveté. As a second-year novice, I worked with a Mexican street gang in Chicago, but I had to leave that ministry because I was in over my head. I was also in danger after witnessing the murder of one of my friends who had left the gang. Then, after the novitiate, during my philosophy studies in Detroit, I got involved with various practices that eventually became known as the New Age movement.

During my regency (i.e., the period after philosophy studies when Jesuit scholastics teach high school or perform some other Jesuit work), I was sent to St. Xavier High School in Cincinnati. I didn't like teaching high school at all! Teaching high school students requires more attention to discipline than to the subject being taught. I neither understood their need for correction nor enjoyed administering discipline. Nonetheless, in His providence, God used this time to give me the opportunity to become involved in the Catholic Charismatic Renewal. Reading Charismatic literature and the works of C. S. Lewis and G. K. Chesterton renewed and cleansed me theologically as I got out of the New Age movement. (I wrote in detail about these experiences in my book *Catholics and the New Age* [Servant Publications, 1992]). Suffice to say, I knew I was not called to the priesthood to summon people to the self-absorption and narcissism inherent in New Age practices.

At the end of two years of (trying my best at) teaching in a high school, I was accepted to study theology at Loyola University in Chicago. And two years after that, in 1976, I was ordained to the priesthood. It was a day of great joy. After eighteen years of working toward the priesthood, I received the laying on of Cardinal Cody's hands and the anointing of my own hands, thereby enabling me to join the other priests in saying the words of consecration. Also, I knew that from that day forward I would be able to continue to preach the Gospel and celebrate Mass for the Church. My life's goal had opened up new horizons for priestly service for the rest of my life. The day of ordination was also one about which my father had warned me a decade earlier.

A FATHER'S PROMISE, A SON'S EXPLANATION

On the day after my ordination, I joined my family in South Haven, Michigan, where they had moved while I was studying philosophy in Detroit. There, I celebrated my first Mass at St. Basil's Church. Guests at the party that followed included my fellow Jesuits, family, childhood friends, friends from the street-gang work, and former high school students. At the end of the dinner my dad took me aside and reminded me, "You know that since you have become a Jesuit priest, you are now out of my will." I accepted his pronouncement with a smile and a nod; given my vows, I knew that I couldn't keep the money anyway.

My path soon led me to graduate work in Old Testament. My spiritual director's suggestion that I pursue Old Testament studies seemed like deep, deep waters that were way over my head. However, such a degree would mean that I could teach at the college level, where classroom discipline would not be much of an issue, while interest in the subject matter would be greatly increased. These prospects made the necessity of swimming through the deep waters a worthwhile task.

I was accepted at Vanderbilt University in Nashville, Tennessee and, after a half-dozen years of struggle (especially for this "C" student from Quigley), I received my Ph.D. in Old Testament in 1984. I also taught there as a graduate assistant, lecturing on Judaism, and taught Old Testament at Tennessee State. Shortly thereafter, God took my apostolic work to places I never imagined.

While at Vanderbilt in Nashville I had met Deacon Bill Steltemeier, a man with whom I would establish a great friendship and who would play a major role in the most significant apostolic work to date. (I will return to this topic a bit later in the story.)

My mom died of cancer in 1989 and my dad died of a heart attack a few years later. They had divorced in the early 1980s, which caused me a lot of pain. Mom and Dad had always been a single unit; I learned of their separation when I paid a surprise visit on Father's Day. No one had told me of it, and the news that Dad was living with another woman absolutely shocked me when I arrived at our house. The heartbreak was in the foreground of my thoughts and feelings for a couple years, and only then faded to the background. Despite the great affect divorce has on a person (even supposed well-adjusted adults), I consider it an answer to prayers that they reconciled with each other just before Mom died, and that Dad was there to help us kids care for her and lay her to rest.

Four years after Mom died, Dad had serious aneurism and heart surgery, just a few months before he passed away. While in the hospital awaiting surgery he called me to his side, told my siblings to leave the room, and asked to go to confession. I offered to find another priest, since he had said previously that he would never confess his sins to me. But no; now he insisted he wanted *me*.

You might think that I would feel a sense of vindication or relief that my father finally accepted me as a priest. But I can honestly say that that was the furthest thing from my mind. God had brought me such a long way from when I barely gave a thought to the feelings of the young lady I had been as dating. Now my concern for people went even deeper than simply human feelings. It went to the very core of life. St. Paul said, "[W]e regard no one from a human point of view," and "we are ambassadors for Christ, God making his appeal through us. We beseech you on behalf of Christ, be reconciled to God" (2 Corinthians 5:20). To me, at that moment, my father was a sinner who needed the love and mercy of God. That was all. I simply desired his soul be healed and that he be prepared for death.

He had a greater sense of peace in his last few months than he had in all his adult years. The words I had spoken to him at age twelve—that I wanted to be a priest to cure souls and help sinners on their death beds to get to heaven—came to be lived out in his own life thirty-two years later. God is good.

Nothing compares to meeting a soul in the sacrament of Reconciliation. There I, a poor sinner yet also a priest of God, have the unspeakable privilege of ministering the very love and mercy of God. There Christ asks me to touch and heal in His Name. If that was the only thing I ever got to do, it would be worth spending my life as a priest. But God's blessings to me have been so much more.

THE WORLD BECOMES MY PULPIT

Shortly after meeting Deacon Steltemeier, he introduced me to a unique religious sisters, whose vision, skill and charm would soon work with the grace of God to create a "network of miracles," as journalist Raymond Arroyo would state some twenty plus years later.

In 1978, God called the deacon (with a little help from Mother Angelica herself) to assist Mother's community of Poor Clares nuns to launch the Eternal Word Television Network (EWTN). Little did anyone know that this ambitious idea would become one of the greatest success stories in Catholic history. Today, EWTN is the world's largest religious network, reaching more than 120 million homes in 144 countries, airing in both English and Spanish. When EWTN aired for the first time on August 15, 1981 Mother Angelica tapped the good deacon to be the president of the new network.

The deacon asked me to do a show with Mother in February 1984. Mother and I hit it off immediately and quickly became great friends. For the next several years I enjoyed being her guest on *Mother Angelica Live* with occasional stints as the guest host of the show. Shortly after finishing a teaching assignment at the University of Dallas in 1999, Mother had a stroke. Deeply loved by hundreds of thousands of people, Mother began a long, challenging recovery. It was during this time that she and Deacon Bill invited me to come to EWTN to assist her full-time. My superiors approved the request just two days before she suffered a second, more debilitating stroke. In God's providence, I was free to go there, where the need was real. I marvel each week at the opportunity this worldwide pulpit has afforded me to preach and teach the Gospel. This opportunity has also reminded me often of the extraordinary responsibility. I thought the pressure to do well was great when I was afforded the chance to attend Quigley forty years before. The opportunity to proclaim and live the Gospel in front of the world is a great way to improve one's spiritual life and reliance on God. I shutter to think I would face this weekly task with my own strength. Both the world and I would be in trouble at that point.

My childhood fantasies of cowboy adventures really did come true. We priests are the "white hat" guys. Just look at our pope. He wears a white hat! Having a leader like John Paul II for most of my priestly life was a blessing and inspiration—I loved being part of his "posse" and could not have been more proud of this great man and his successor, Benedict XVI. What great teachers and leaders God has given to the Church!

When God calls a man to be a priest, it is to take nothing from him, and gives him everything his heart desires—even things he could not desire. I give thanks to God—here and in eternity—for affording me this glorious vocation.

৯৯

ACKNOWLEDGMENTS

First and foremost, we would like to thank Jesus Christ, the Priest, for the incomprehensible gift of His Presence. Through His Presence the ministry of the ordained priesthood is gifted to all humanity. Through His priests we are baptized, forgiven and blessed into the communion of our one Heavenly Father as adopted sons and daughters.

We would like to express our deep gratitude to every man who has made his life an offering to the People of God as one of His chosen priests. Your daily "yes" in fidelity to His divine call is appreciated: you are needed and loved by us all.

Many thanks as well to the staff and associates of Ascension Press, particularly its president, Matthew Pinto, and managing editor, Michael Flickinger, for their enthusiastic and unfailing support of this project.

Christine Anne Mugridge:
I would particularly like to remember several devout and noble men of God whose candor, insight, wisdom and model of holiness impacted my life greatly: Msgr. George Monaghan, Fr. Charles Kubsz (Camaldolese Congregation of the Order of St. Benedict), Fr. Ray Ryland, Fr. Abbot Joseph Homick, Fr. Gary Sumpter, Fr. John Corapi, SOLT, and especially Fr. James Flanagan, SOLT.

Jerry Usher:
I would like to thank Pope John Paul II, a hero of mine in every sense of the word. While my disappointments in life have

been few, one will always be never having had the opportunity
to fulfill the dream of meeting him in person (though, thanks be
to God, I did see him on several occasions). But I'm sure when
finally we do meet in heaven, it will be far better.

Finally, we extend a concluding word of gratitude to those
priests whose stories are shared in this anthology—without
whom this book would not be a reality. Your witness to Christ
and His priesthood inspires us daily.

ABOUT THE EDITORS

Dr. Christine Anne Mugridge received her doctorate in social communications and theology from the Pontifical University of the Salesians in Rome. The focus of her work is the *Theology of Communication and the New Evangelization.* She is the Rome correspondent/producer for Relevant Radio and former host of the EWTN radio program *Off the Shelf,* as well as the author of *God's Call to Women* (Servant, 2003). Christine presently serves as assistant to Fr. James Flanagan, SOLT, Founder of the Society of Our Most Holy Trinity in Rome.

Jerry Usher is the creator and host of *Catholic Answers Live,* a call-in talk show that airs on over one hundred stations nationally and on Sirius Satellite Radio and the Internet. He recently founded Third Millennium Media, an apostolate dedicated to helping Catholic radio stations enhance their on-air presentation and other apostolates establish a presence in Catholic media. He is a fourth degree member of the Knights of Columbus, and a past Grand Knight and Deputy Grand Knight of Council No. 7792 in San Diego.